I0493362

Workplace Solutions:
Exploring Conflict Resolution and
Dealing with Difficult People

Helene Malmsio

Workplace Solutions: Exploring Conflict Resolution and Dealing with Difficult People

Copyright © 2014 by Helene Malmsio

ISBN-13: 978-1497304277
ISBN-10: 149730427X

Table of Contents

Introduction

In any workplace environment you're bound to have disagreements that lead to conflict. And just about every person also experiences dealing with difficult people in the office. If you're experiencing a lot of workplace conflict or have to deal with people who frustrate you, this book will teach you how to manage those situations.

Here you'll learn what causes conflict and the different types of conflict that you can encounter. You'll also learn how your own conflict style effects what's going on in your environment.

In addition, you'll find strategies for improving communication so that you no longer have to dread talking with coworkers and leaders in your institution. There are many ways you can prevent conflict from ever getting started.

And when conflict does arise, you'll learn how you can use it to your benefit rather than give into office drama. The truth is that you need to have relationships with coworkers. Very few businesses actually operate without some sort of teamwork.

It can be difficult to work with people who have a wide variety of points of view. But when you learn some communication skills and develop company norms that promote positive interactions you can take all those ideas and make them into a stronger team.

Even with the best of communication skills, you'll still find that you have to deal with people who are unreasonable at times. There are many reasons that people exhibit difficult behavior and we'll take a look at some of the most common reasons.

If you find yourself faced with a difficult person, you'll need to have a tried and true strategy. In this book you'll find a 5 step process for dealing with difficult people that can help you smooth over the situation.

Ultimately, the only person you can control is yourself. You'll learn how you can make changes in your own thinking and behavior that make it possible to have better communication. Not only will this improve your life in the office, it can extend to making all of your relationships better.

If you've struggled with conflict, managing your anger, and dealing with difficult people you'll get the information you need to get relief from the struggle and instead thrive. Let's begin by looking at what conflict is and how it can affect us.

Chapter 1: What is Conflict?

There's not a person alive who hasn't experienced conflict. You may have your own definition of what conflict is. But it's important to clarify what it means in the context of this guide.

In an organization, conflict is anything that disrupts your normal routine. It can also involve hostility that arises when people are working for different outcomes and interfere with each other's work.

You may want to spend some time thinking about what conflict means to you and what happens in your workplace. There can be more than one definition, but we'll be working with the definition above as we move through this guide.

Myths About Conflict

When dealing with conflict, there are many myths that organizations and managers have. Making these assumptions can lead to bigger problems down the road. Let's take a look at some common myths.

Conflict is avoidable.

Conflict really isn't avoidable. It's going to occur any time you have people with different personality types working together. By assuming it can be avoided or that people should just "cut it out" managers can actually breed conflict.

Conflict creates polarization.

Many people just want conflict to go away. They believe that having conflict can completely polarize an entire organization and has no benefit. While it's true that conflict can be destructive, it can also be constructive.

Conflict creates inappropriate reactions.

While some people have inappropriate reactions to conflict, there are also many people with appropriate actions. There are times when disagreement can be handled in very appropriate ways.

Think, for example, about a referee at a sporting event. Two coaches or teammates may disagree about a particular play.

The referee's job is to look at the evidence and make a determination. No one in this example has to use inappropriate behavior.

And, of course, we've all seen inappropriate reactions in a sporting event when two players get into a physical fight or fans boo at the teams. This type of behavior is inappropriate.

But the conflict isn't necessarily the problem – the choices of individuals to do inappropriate things is really about personal responsibility.

Constructive vs. Destructive Conflict

Conflict can serve two purposes. It can help people to see a different point of view and actually create positive change or it can cause relationships and work to become disrupted and create negative change.

Constructive conflict can:

- Encourage creativity

- Open you up to new points of view

- Lead to better decision-making

- Clear the air

These are good things that can and should happen in a team work environment. It's always good to think outside your own perspective and share ideas. There's great value in understanding different points of view.

Destructive conflict can:

- Damage relationships

- Disrupt your work routine

- Increase expenses

- Cause people to leave work that they actually enjoy

- Lead to bad business decisions

- Create barriers that weren't there before

When you have destructive conflict in the workplace, you have a big problem. The idea here is that you can learn to have differing points of view without creating a hostile work environment.

Working with Conflict

The idea here is that you don't need to eliminate conflict. In fact you can't actually do that. Instead, you need to learn how you can use conflict to your advantage in your business.

Different points of view can breed amazing inventions, business plans, and allow creativity and innovation to soar. It's important to embrace the positive parts of conflict and then learn how to keep the destructive conflict at bay.

As you read on you'll learn more about how you can create an environment where conflict is allowed to improve your workplace rather than tear it down. Many people don't understand how to make conflict work to their advantage.

It's not surprising that a lot of the conflict in an office becomes destructive and makes everyone miserable. But even if you've experienced terrible problems with conflict, it's not too late to turn the ship around.

How Has Conflict Affected You?

Throughout this guide you'll be asked to reflect on how the things we discuss relate to you. Consider the following:

- Have you experienced conflict at work?

- Think of an example of conflict that was negative.

- Consider a time when conflict actually helped inspire creativity and improve your work.

- Do you try to avoid conflict or welcome it as part of working on a team?

As you continue to read, you'll learn strategies for understanding the causes of conflict and being able to embrace it to create a more powerful business.

Chapter 2: Understanding Different Types of Conflict

There's actually more than one type of conflict. How you manage conflict will be dependent up on the type with which you're dealing. In this chapter we'll discuss three types of conflict. We'll also look at open versus hidden conflict.

Three Types of Conflict

Research has actually determined that conflict can be broken down into three types: inner conflict, interpersonal conflict, and group conflict. It's important to understand each type.

Inner Conflict.

Inner conflict may be something you find hard to recognize. However, this type of conflict is the most common and the most difficult to experience. Basically this is the idea that you're conflicted about something in your own mind.

Usually this is brought on by questions of what you value, your ethics, and your integrity. It's about doing what's right opposed to doing what you want to do. There are many ways this can show up in life. Let's take a look at some possible examples:

- You've set a goal at work that will decrease your amount of time at home with your family. You feel conflicted about what's right.

- You've already put in a 50 hour work week, but there's a presentation regarding an important issue you've been asked to attend. You feel exhausted, but your conscience says you should go.

- You've been invited to apply for a promotion that would give you a better salary and you feel confident you can do the job, but you're nervous about applying because you may fail. You're conflicted about whether or not to apply.

- You disagree with your boss on a decision. You feel that there may be something you can do to change things, but you're also concerned about voicing your opinion and causing problems at work.

All of these situations are really about your internal dialogue. You have good reasons for wanting to choose 2 different options.

There are actually different subcategories of reactions to inner conflict. Let's take a look at 10 different inner conflict reactions with examples of each.

Reaction #1 – Compensation.

This is caused when a person feels the need to make up for inadequacy – real or imagined. An example of this might be working hard for a social club as a leader to make up for what you feel you lack in your career.

Reaction #2 – Conversion.

This is when your emotional conflicts are actually expressed physically in the form of pain, muscle tension, or other symptoms. For example, a person who has worked hard on a valued project finds himself with a terrible headache when that project is rejected by his boss.

Reaction #3 – Displacement.

Displacement is a reaction caused by pent- up emotions that end up being taken out on a person, idea, or object that isn't really the primary source. For example, if you're having a tough time with your boss and take out your frustrations on a coworker.

Reaction #4 – Fantasy.

With fantasy you might end up daydreaming or finding other imaginative ways to escape from your reality. You may imagine a world that's more satisfying. You might daydream of having a different boss or actually being the boss.

Reaction #5 –Negativism.

This consists of resistance that's either passive or active. This isn't something that you consciously do, rather an unconscious pattern.

An example of this would be having to attend a meeting you don't want to attend and then picking apart everyone's suggestions.

Reaction #6 – Rationalization.

Rationalization means justifying inappropriate behaviors by trying to provide an acceptable explanation.

For example, padding your expense account at work because "everybody does it".

Reaction #7 – Regression.

Regression occurs when you become less mature and reverts to lesser responsibilities in response to frustration.

For example, if you don't get the promotion you wanted you might start spending more time on clerical work instead of your actual responsibilities.

Reaction #8 – Repression.

If you experience repression, you might cut off your experiences, feelings, and impulses that are disturbing because they cause you to feel bad about yourself or cause anxiety.

For example, you might "forget" to tell your boss about an embarrassing situation because you've blocked it from your mind.

Reaction #9 – Resignation, Apathy, and Boredom.

This reaction is quite common in an employee that isn't happy at work. If you react in this way, you hold back any personal or emotional involvement.

You simply don't care whether or not you do a good job. Usually this is a result of not receiving any praise, reward, or encouragement for the work that you do.

Reaction #10 – Flight or Withdrawal.

If you react with flight or withdrawal, you're likely to leave your job or even your career as a result of experiencing conflict or anxiety. You may also isolate yourself.

For example, if you're unhappy with an experience with your boss you might take the day off. Or you might isolate yourself from coworkers and become a loner.

All of these reactions are unhealthy responses to conflict. Instead of actually dealing with the situation in an assertive and appropriate way, you try to avoid it with unhealthy responses that don't actually resolve the problem.

In fact many of these responses actually create more problems for you personally or in your work environment. The good news is that you can learn a different way.

Interpersonal Conflict.

Interpersonal conflict involves conflict between two or more people. It can be the result of many different issues. Some of the possible causes include:

- Personality clashes
- Value clashes

- Culture clashes

- Communication breakdown

- Workplace policies or traditions that actually lead to conflict

In general, it's easier to get along with someone who is like us. That's because we can understand their behavior better. But when someone has a different set of values beliefs, or thought processes, we simply don't understand them as well.

There are 11 roots of personal conflict. These are differences that lead to conflict between people. As we explore each one of these, think about experiences in your own life that have been examples.

Root Cause #1 – Prejudice/Bias.

Sometimes problems can occur in the workplace simply because based on how one person feels about the other. It has nothing to do with really having different ideas.

Root Cause #2 –Nastiness/Stubbornness.

If an individual has a personal chip on her shoulder, she may go through life looking to create conflict. This may be more comfortable that getting along and agreeing.

Root Cause #3 – Sensitivity/Hurt.

Low self-esteem, insecurity, or conflict in his personal life might lead to a person feeling attacked in the face of criticism. He may see criticism as a statement about who he is rather than a specific mistake.

Root Cause #4 – Differences in Perception/Values.

Everyone has their own perspective of the world around them. Differences in perception and values such as culture, race, experience, socio-economic status, and occupation can result in conflict.

Root Cause #5 – Differences Over Facts.

Facts are statements that can be quantified and verified. Usually when people argue over facts, it's a short argument as it's easy to verify data.

But when someone claims a fact that can't be documented, it can lead to conflict. For example, saying, "It's a fact that you don't care about my feelings," is not constructive and leads to conflict.

Root Cause #6 – Differences Over Goals/Priorities.

Often conflict arises when two or more people have different ideas about what should be the workplace goals or priorities. For example, one person may want to focus more energy on training staff while another person thinks more energy and resources should go to marketing efforts.

Root Cause #7 – Competition for Resources.

When the budget or resources of a company are very limited, two people might argue over how they should be allocated. This is very common in small businesses or nonprofits.

Root Cause #8 – Differences Over Methods.

You may be able to agree with your coworkers about goals, but you may have a hard time agreeing about how you should proceed to meet them.

Root Cause #9 – Competition for Supremacy.

When one person wants to have more attention and outshine others, this can lead to conflict. A common example is two employees who are competing for a promotion.

Root Cause #10 – Misunderstanding.

Sometimes conflict is really about miscommunication. If you're not careful about how you say what you mean and checking for understanding, you can end up with conflict.

Root Cause #11 – Unfulfilled Expectations.

While we often try not to have too many expectations, it's impossible not to have any. And it's often important to have expectations as long as both parties understand and agree to them.

Unfulfilled expectations often lead to conflict in the workplace and in personal situations. That's usually the result of expectations being inappropriate, unreasonable, or just unstated.

Group Conflict.

The third general type of conflict is group conflict. This occurs when there are conflicts between groups such as two different departments in a business.

One department may find the other department's expectations unreasonable.

This type of conflict will be exacerbated by a situation when managers of departments have interpersonal conflict as well. Here are a few examples of causes of group conflict:

- Different goals

- Mutual department independence

- Unequal department dependence

- Dissatisfaction with roles

- Ambiguity of roles

- Inadequate reward systems

- Dependence on common resources

- Barriers to communication

Let's take a look at eight basic causes of group conflict that can occur so that you can relate to how it works in your own work-place.

Goal Segmentation and Rewards.

This is related to differences in goals by departments. For example, different departments have different goals for inventory levels.

Mutual Department Dependence.

This is when the success of one department depends on another. For example, the sales for the marketing department are dependent on how much the production department can manufacture.

Unequal Departmental Dependence.

This occurs when one department is dependent on another, but other departments don't share that dependence. For example, the staff departments are usually more dependent on line departments.

Functional Unit and Environment.

Within an organization, there are usually different environments and cultures. For example, the marketing department may have less structure than the accounting department.

Role Dissatisfaction.

Often there are departments that collectively feel their contributions aren't recognized.

Role Ambiguities.

This occurs when it's unclear which department is responsible for specific tasks. When a success or failure happens, it's impossible to determine which department actually had the assignment.

Common Resource Dependence.

This is common when departments share resources such as computers and meeting rooms. There may be conflict over which department gets more time with these resources.

Communication Barriers.

Often there can be differences between departments when it comes to language. The engineering department may use a different vocabulary than the sales department for the same things.

Open Conflict vs. Hidden Conflict

There are two ways that we can deal with conflict. We can be open and up front about it or we can keep it hidden where it will often stew and grow.

Open Conflict.

Open conflict is actually much easier to deal with than hidden conflict. When you know what the problems are, you can actually work to do something about them.

Open conflict is most likely to arise due to:

- Differing assumptions, perceptions, and miscommunications. Speaking openly about this conflict gives opportunities to get clarification and clear up confusion. It also gives you the chance to get to know others' views.

- Different behavior patterns, management styles, and interpersonal problems can get in the way of moving toward common goals or collaborating as you need to. This gives the opportunity to discuss differences, improve relationships, and create trust.

- Conflicts of goals. These give the opportunity to discuss different opinions about goals and work to arrive at a similar place.

The good think about open conflict is that you can discuss the issues, get everything out in the air, and work toward solutions. Eventually most people are able to work out a compromise that both parties can live with.

Hidden Conflict.

With hidden conflict, it's more difficult to address problems because they aren't always obvious. It may not even be known in someone who's experiencing inner conflict.

With this type of conflict, there isn't the opportunity to talk about problems and iron out solutions. This can lead to problems with sabotage and decrease productivity. If an organization is experiencing hidden conflict, it can be very difficult to determine what's causing changes in productivity.

What Type of Conflict Have You Experienced?

It's important to consider conflict you've experienced in the past as well as conflict that might plague you personally or in the workplace.

- Can you think of an example of inner conflict, interpersonal conflict, and group conflict that you've experienced?

- When have you experienced hidden conflict? When have you experienced open conflict?

- Does your workplace seem to have a great deal of conflict? What type(s)?

As you continue moving through this guide keep those examples in mind.

There are people who speak without putting much thought into their words and don't consider the consequences before they act. This type of behavior is known as spontaneous action.

On the flipside, there are those who are very cautious before they speak. These people tend to be introverted and sometimes they think so much that they don't actually take any action. This type of person is more comfortable with reflective action.

The best place to be is somewhere in the middle of these two. You want to be thoughtful about consequences, but it's also important to speak up for yourself and take action when needed.

Unfortunately, many people don't really understand their own behaviors or the effects they have on others. But becoming aware of how your behavior affects others is essential to resolving conflict.

The Johari Window

The Johari Window is a technique that you can use to determine the effect of your behavior on others. This tool was created by two men named Joseph Luft and Harrington Ingham.

The following illustrates that there are certain things you know about yourself and certain things that you don't. At the same time there are things that others know about you and certain things they don't know about you. They may know things about you that you don't even know yourself.

	Known to Others	Not Known to Others
Known to Oneself	Open	Partially Open
Not Known to Oneself	Partially Open	Hidden

It's important to become more aware of the effect of your behavior on others. There are basically two major ways that you can do this. You can use the diagram to illustrate how much is known about you – both by yourself and others.

Window 1 involves things that are known to oneself and known to others. This is the most open understanding of behavior.

Window 2 is information about your behavior that's know to you, but it's known to others. This condition is called partially open.

In window 3 you find understandings about your behavior that aren't known to you, but are known to others. This is also considered partially open.

The final window 4 is understanding that isn't known to you or to others. This is called hidden.

Listen to Yourself.

The first way you can become more aware is just by listening to yourself. Consider how you're reacting and feeling. At the same time, consider what might be causing those reactions and feelings.

This requires you to be more thoughtful of your everyday actions and feelings. Many people tend to ignore their feelings and how they react to the world. But in order to have better communication, you must become more self-aware.

Request Feedback.

The second way you can become aware of how you affect others is to actually ask. When you ask for feedback, you can find out how they see you and what they think about your behavior.

Building relationships with other people involves moving toward more open windows. This is the process of getting to know your own behavior as well as understanding how others react to it.

The idea is that the more information is known by you and known to others, the clearer you'll be able to communicate with others. You need to work to expand your open windows and eliminate your hidden or blind areas.

You can reduce your hidden area by sharing more about your-self. This helps people to understand you better.

At the same time, you can encourage others to be more open with you. This helps everyone become more self-aware and experience better communication.

Relationship Styles

You can actually use the Johari Windows idea and apply it to styles of human communication and relations. Let's take a look at some examples of how this works with characterizations using animals.

The Turtle.

A person who is considered a "turtle" is someone who has low trust and low respect. They aren't very forthcoming with their feelings and they're also not interested in listening to others.

This is someone who has low respect for the opinions of others and has low trust in their motives. This isn't usually a conscious decision, rather something that is done unconsciously.

There can be many problems with this type of person. They can experience misunderstandings, unresolved problems, frustra-tion, and actually miss out on opportunities for creativity.

If you're in a relationship with someone you might feel that the relationship is cold, unsatisfying, and very impersonal. And while two people can be involved a "turtle" relationship, they can also exist between groups of people.

There could be turtle relationships between divisions in a company, between managers and their employees, or between an organization and the public. This usually leads to problems with morale and poor performance. Obviously this is a type of relationship that needs to change.

The good news is that these relationships can improve with conscious effort. If people decide to become willing and open to listen to the ideas and feelings of others, and they also are willing to be vulnerable and share their own thoughts and feelings, the relationship can be healed.

However, both parties have to be willing to take the chance and open up in order for it to work. This takes someone who is brave enough or fed up enough to begin opening the lines of communication and requires the other party to step up as well.

The Owl.

The owl is actually a little better than the turtle because he actually respects the opinion of others. The owl shows openness to other's ideas and feelings. But, the owl doesn't share his own feelings or ideas.

This is someone who has high respect for others, but low trust in them. Avoiding self-expression can be very unsatisfying because it causes a one-way relationship to develop.

Neither partner is actually very satisfied by this relationship. But there can be progress if the owl makes the decision to begin sharing information and feelings. This shows that he trusts the other person in the relationship and leads to better communication overall.

As the owl becomes more open, the relationship improves. But it's difficult for someone to become more open and it usually happens gradually. Being open and honest can make one feel vulnerable and can feel very scary.

The situation is helped if the partner is very open and respectful when it comes to listening to ideas and feelings that are shared by the owl. But not listening or showing criticism can actually cause the owl to become closed off again.

The Bull in the China Shop.

The bull in the china shop is happy to share feelings and ideas, but isn't good at listening to what others are saying or taking care with their feelings. This is someone who has high trust in others, but low respect for their opinions.

The bull's willingness to share shows that he trusts the person he's talking to. But his inability to listen to others makes people feel that they are unimportant. This is another type of one-sided relationship that can cause problems.

When people feel that their opinions and feelings don't matter, they develop negative feelings. They can have low self-esteem or eventually turn away from the bull completely.

In order for this situation the bull has to decide to become a better listener and then work on this skill. In order to arrive at that conclusion, he'll have to realize that there's a problem and that other people have opinions and feelings that matter.

But if he does this, he can begin listening and improve the relationships both in the workplace and at home.

The Picture Window.

The most effective style of communication is the picture window. With this relationship style, the person is open and willing to share her feelings. At the same time, she listens and is interested in the ideas, feelings, and opinions of others.

This style lends itself to mutual respect and an ease. This style encourages free discussion and sharing of ideas. When there is conflict, it's seen as an opportunity to understand each other better rather than a problem.

Disagreement is a natural part of life, but if you can be open to understanding each other conflict can actually improve relationships rather than tear them down.

What Does Your Window Look Like?

Take a few moments and think about your own Johari Window. Where do you think you stand?

- Do you ask for feedback about your own behavior and how it affects others?

- Are you open to listening to others?

- Do you share your own thoughts, feelings, and opinions?

Think about your own relationships. You may have different styles for different relationships. What style do you think you have in your personal life with friends? What are your relationships like with coworkers or your boss?

Do you need to work on sharing more about your own thoughts? Do you need to be more respectful and listen to others more? By really getting honest with yourself about these questions you can make improvements in your relationships.

Ultimately, in order to have positive relationships and conflict that results in constructive activities, you want to strive for a picture window relationship.

Chapter 4: The Five Stages of Conflict

Conflict isn't one of those things that is "on" or "off". It actually has stages and levels that cause tensions to build until there are problems. In this chapter we'll look at two different ways to look at conflict.

It's important to understand these phases because it can help you to resolve conflict in early stages when there is less resentment and tension. As a manager, it's especially important to understand these stages.

The Five Stages of Conflict

This model is one way of looking at conflict that shows how tensions can build and what happens when there isn't a positive intervention. Conflict can quickly escalate into its destructive form.

Latent Conflict.

At this stage of conflict, there are conditions that are ripe for conflict to arise but they haven't been noticed yet. There are many conditions that could lead to conflict, but in general anything that keeps basic communication from being open and honest can lead to latent conflict.

Differences in culture, race, gender, and socioeconomic status can lead to latent conflict. There's also a potential for this type of conflict when there is a power differential such as with a boss and employee.

Perceived Conflict.

In the case of perceived conflict, one or both of the people engaged in conflict recognizes its cause. There are many reasons that conflict can arise.

But one example is coworkers who are also friends. One of them gets a promotion and the other feels slighted. This can lead to the seeds of conflict.

Felt Conflict.

With felt conflict, we begin to see the conflict escalate and tensions build. There isn't an actual struggle at this point, but the possibility of conflict is greatly increasing.

For example, two coworkers who are short-tempered with each other or friends who bicker are experiencing felt conflict.

While there hasn't been a major problem yet, it's very easy for this to set the stage for big disagreements and destructive conflict.

Manifest Conflict.

Manifest conflict indicates that conflict is happening and obvious to those who aren't involved. There may be arguments and hurt feelings that are no longer being kept hidden.

This type of conflict can lead to disruptions that occur in any environment. For example, seeing a husband and wife in a public argument or observing a teenager rebelling against her parents. You can also see arguments in the office between coworkers or between a boss and employee.

Conflict Aftermath.

When conflict has ended, we're in the stage of conflict aftermath. Conflict can end as a result of actual resolution or by suppression. If conflict is dealt with in a constructive way, there can be a decrease in future conflict.

But if you're in a situation where the conflict has ended because feelings were suppressed instead of dealt with, you actually create even more tension. This can lead to major conflict problems including:

- Firings

- End of a friendship

- Divorce

- Partnerships ended

- Future destructive conflict

All of these are examples of poor conflict resolution. It's important that you try to end conflicts with positive resolutions. This can bring relationships closer together and help partnerships become stronger.

Being able to discuss opinions and feelings and improve communication can only help a relationship. This is what is meant by constructive conflict. It's actually a good thing to be open and honest and disagree. But the way you handle those disagreements can make or break the relationship.

When we think of these stages, it's important to note that they don't always go in order and you don't always experience every stage. You can jump in at any point depending on the situation and behavior.

The Struggle Spectrum

The struggle spectrum is another way of looking at conflict. This shows the progression from calm and peaceful discussions to arguments that lead to fighting and even war. Let's take a look at this version of conflict progression.

Stage 1: Mild Difference.

This first stage includes differences, but those are usually just differences in interests. People who exit conflict at this stage are generally able to discuss their differences with good will.

They are open and forthright about their feelings and opinions. At the same time, they're able to listen to and accept others' points of view. When this happens, conflict is very limited and constructive.

But it's common for people to begin with a mild difference that begins to escalate when not resolved positively.

Stage 2: Disagreement.

If a mild difference isn't resolved positively it can grow into a disagreement. A mild difference might be put aside and even forgotten.

Or it could be stored in your memory until you need it in the future. You can also avoid mild differences.

But mild differences can also escalate and turn into disagreements. The mild difference goes from mild to a bit more intense. Two parties may have more interaction around the differences they have.

In the beginning, both parties may be working toward problem solving and resolving differences. But if they can't come to an agreement they may begin to negotiate with each other. At this point they're still trying to reach a mutual agreement.

However, this type of communication doesn't always work to solve the problem. The two parties may find that they're stuck in a stalemate and can't reach an agreement. This leads to the next stage of conflict.

Stage 3: Dispute.

If you're unable to resolve a disagreement, it can be become more intense and turn into an all-out dispute. The discussions around the disagreement can now become heated rather than cordial.

You may begin to see each other in a more negative light and the discussion can become more polarized with each party getting further and further apart. This can lead to problem such as shouting, making accusations, and being spiteful toward one another.

This stage usually includes intense arguments as well as bargaining. Bargaining may sound nice, but in this context it's about arguing, threatening, making proposals and counterproposals. But the object is usually to obtain goals that are mutually exclusive.

A dispute can be resolved if both parties are willing to give up on some of their points. But communication at this point can be very tense and limited which makes it difficult to resolve this type of conflict.

You can see this type of conflict occur between two people, two departments, two businesses, and even two countries.

Stage 4: Campaign.

If a dispute is unresolved, the next stage is campaign or litigation. With this stage, the struggle continues to grow larger and now begins to involve more participants.

Each party in the dispute tries to gain supporters and campaigns for votes. This moves to more of a political struggle with each party working to persuade others to take their side.

You may see media engaged and literature begin to be used such as pamphlets or books. You may also see a mass rally be developed in order to persuade many people to take action. At this point, it becomes much more difficult to compromise.

Agreements are usually seen as weakness – this is a win or lose situation. Instead of communicating with each other, parties in disagreement speak more to their supporters. The walls become much higher and thicker between the original parties with the disagreement.

Does this remind you of political campaigns or even disputes between countries? This type of escalation can lead to major problems such as rioting.

Stage 5: Litigation.

Legal action is an alternative stage that doesn't always occur. This is when a dispute is taken through legal processes to get resolution. There are two different levels of the litigation phase – arbitration and proceeding to court.

Arbitration is a less formal type of litigation and going to court is more formal. With this type of action, the decision making is taken away from the parties and given to a third party.

In the corporate environment we see this frequently with labor relations when employees and management can't agree to terms.

Stage 6: Fight and/or War.

This is when conflict escalates to the highest level. This stage is characterized by violence and destruction. At this point we have two parties who can't resolve differences and instead choose to try to eliminate the other. This is common in international relationships such as the war between the US and Iraq.

While communication isn't healthy at this stage, it isn't absent. Communicating with a punch, a gun, or a bomb sets a clear message.

However, the only intervention that can change things is physical, psychological, or economic force. In any case this involves in the destruction of at least one of the parties, but often there's an element of this for both.

Are You in a Conflict Stage?

We've all experienced conflict as it's a natural and healthy part of life. Take a few moments and consider your own relationships and conflict stages. Have you been able to stay in the milder stages or have you experienced escalation?

If you've had success resolving conflict before it escalates, what type of communication did you engage in? What made the process more friendly?

If you've had conflict become destructive and lead to contention and fights, what has led to that place? Were there things you could have done to prevent that stage of conflict?

You may recognize that things went wrong, but have a hard time pinpointing exactly when and how.

Ultimately we want to have conflict that leads to growth, closer relationships, and the ability to work together in harmony. In the next chapter we'll look at different outcomes that are possible with conflict.

And as you continue, you'll learn how you can be a facilitator for positive communication and help conflicts get resolved in constructive and healthy ways.

Chapter 5: The Results of Conflict

Conflict wouldn't be such a big deal if it didn't come with serious consequences. There are basically three different possible outcomes for conflict, but only one of them is actually healthy and the result of good conflict resolution skills.

Let's begin with taking a look at the three different possible outcomes and then we'll look at strategies for dealing with each one.

Lose-Lose

When you avoid conflict or try to smooth things over without actually getting everything out in the open, you can end up with a lose-lose situation. In this outcome, no one really gets what they want or need and the underlying problems that led to the conflict are never resolved.

That can lead to future conflict that's very similar. If you don't resolve issues they have a way of rearing their ugly heads again and again. You may think that you can avoid conflict by suppressing the issues, but this doesn't work in reality.

When you avoid your conflict, you pretend it doesn't exist and hope that it goes away on its own. Smoothing things over is the act of downplaying the differences between parties.

Compromising sounds good in theory, but it can set the stage for future problems as well. By compromising, both parties end up giving up some of their desires. While it can help to move forward in the short-term, it doesn't resolve all of the problems.

Instead, the conflict seems to be settled but the deep issues that caused it to occur in the first place can reappear in the future. This happens a lot with unions and management in the corporate setting. While a contract may be negotiated, when the contract is up the same issues come up again.

Win-Lose

In a win-lose situation, one party gets what they want, but in doing so keep the other party from being able to achieve all of their desires. This can be the result of a contest or competition where there's a winner and a loser.

This situation is also common when there's an authoritative person or party in command. The authority makes the decision while the other party simply has to accept that resolution. When there is a party that's in authority, it's obvious who will get what they want and who might lose out.

This doesn't solve any of the root causes of conflict and instead allows them to fester.

Eventually those issues will probably recur and the conflict will happen all over again. In the case of a corporation, this type of situation may cause employees to leave and seek work in places where they can be heard and have their desires met.

Win-Win

Win-win conflict is the best possible outcome. In this situation healthy problem solving techniques are used to help both parties work out their differences. To have a win-win outcome, there has to be a positive approach to conflict resolution and problem solving.

With this outcome, the conflict is really resolved. It won't be hidden away only to come back later. That's because every party gets what it needs.

Ultimately, a win-win solution results in parties being able to say:

- I want to solve this difference in a way that achieves your goals as well as my goals. I want it to be acceptable to both of us.

- It is the responsibility of all parties to be open and honest about the facts of the situation as well as our opinions and feelings.

- I want to listen to your point of view and really understand it so that we can develop a solution together.

When all parties have these outcomes in mind, you have the best likelihood of improving the situation and allowing everyone to part in a healthy, satisfied way.

Avoidance Leads to Poor Outcomes

It's important to understand that the worst way to deal with conflict is to avoid it. Suppressing feelings and opinions will almost always lead to escalation of the stages of conflict and result in a lose-lose outcome.

Research has shown that the best outcomes come from approaches using problem-solving and even confrontation. Confrontation can be scary for some, but it gets the issues on the table so that real problem-solving can take place.

In research, organizations that have more confrontation actually have better performance in their specific markets. Within an organization, a manager that is more confrontational will also be identified as someone who fosters constructive conflict.

Confronting doesn't mean being aggressive or rude. It simply means being able to discuss an issue instead of allowing things to go unsaid.

As you go throughout your own work life and even personal life, it's helpful to remember this key point.

Strategies for Dealing with Conflict

When you have two parties working together in any capacity, there is the potential for conflict. And if those parties don't come up with solutions, eventually both of them will lose out in the end. T he results of conflict can be positive or negative, but it depends on how the people involved choose to handle the situation.

There are many different strategies for dealing with conflict, some healthy and some not. For example:

- Smoothing over the disagreement

- Withdrawing from the situation

- Compromising

- Enforcing a solution

- Confronting the problem directly

And conflict management approaches can fit into one of three categories – win/lose strategies, lose/lose strategies, or win/win strategies. We'll talk about each one of these in detail.

Win/Lose Strategies.

A win/lose strategies has one party achieving goals at the expense of the other party. This is a short-term solution and usually doesn't take care of the underlying problem that caused the conflict in the first place.

If one person loses while the other wins, there is likely to be resentment. Often applying this approach actually sets the stage for future conflict. There are two ways that this type of strategy is generally used in a workplace environment.

Manager Rules –

The first way it can be used is the manager acts as the authority. He or she will decide how the problem will be solved and have the final say. In this case, there may not be any feedback or discussion from those who are involved in the conflict.

There can also the possibility of the manager giving threats to the security of others by telling them they can do what they're instructed to do of risk losing their job. This puts an end to any questioning or debate.

Majority Rules –

Another option is to take a vote. In this case, the majority rules and that will make the final decision. Unless everyone casts the same vote, there are going to be people who lose with this type of decision making.

When is this used?

Most often the win/lose strategies are used when a solution can't be found or parties can't even talk to each other. When work isn't going on because of conflict, a manager may decide that it's time to just make a decision and move on.

The concern here isn't about maintaining a good morale or communication; it's about the bottom line. Of course, when you don't get everything out in the open you can expect to have to deal with this situation again.

Lose/Lose Strategies.

A lose/lose strategy might be used to eliminate conflicts, though no one really gets what they want. This strategy is not as desirable as others might be, but it can sometimes be used just to end a conflict in the short term. There are three general ways that this strategy is used in the real world.

Compromise –

One lose/lose strategy used in conflict resolution is compromising. Both parties can be asked to give up something that they desire in order to reach an acceptable agreement. In this case both parties may feel that they've lost.

Arbitrator –

An arbitrator is a third party person who can make the decision about how the conflict will be resolved. Instead of the parties coming to an agreement, a compromise is imposed upon them.

An arbitrator will hear both sides and then make a decision about what is best moving forward. Both parties may lose something in the process in order to reach a settlement and move on.

Going by the Rules –

Going by the rules is another way to resolve conflict. This doesn't take anyone's point of view into account; it sees things as more black or white. For example, if an employee asks for a special work schedule due to family obligations, the manager may have to go back to the handbook to the rule.

It's lose/lose because the employee has not gotten their needs met personally and the manager may then lose some productivity from her employee.

When is this used?

Most often this is used when time is of the essence. If there isn't time to work through the problem with positive communication, it may be necessary to reach a quick solution in which no party really gets all that they want.

This can cut short a debate that could cause disruption or make the work environment difficult. However, because no one really gets what they want in many ways this just delays more conflict instead of solving problems well.

Win/Win Strategies.

The win/win solution is always the best because it fixes the problem. It's not used to blame, control, or take away any party's desires. With this strategy every party gets to share a point of view.

This creates trust between all parties and everyone can work together to solve the problem in a way that makes everyone happy. There also has to be the basic belief that the problem will be solved based on facts and merit rather than personalities and politics.

True win/win strategy requires a leader that is flexible and patient. He or she has to be willing to listen to all sides and make sure that they feel heard. This person must also stay calm and make sure that no one feels disrespected or dismissed.

The result of this type of strategy is a solution to the problem that resolves the conflict. With a win/win strategy you won't expect to see the same issue come up again because everyone involved has really gotten what they desire.

It can be hard to be the type of leader needed for this strategy. But you can learn the set of skills you need. If you can let go of the need to win or have power, you'll find that it becomes much easier to resolve conflict.

It requires you to put aside your urge to compete and to lay down your pride. But if you do that, you can have a sincere dialogue and create trust even in the midst of disagreement.

This strategy helps everyone to have higher self-esteem and self-respect and in turn helps them to respect the others involved.

When Have You Experienced These Strategies?

Have you ever been a part of a win/win strategy for conflict resolution? It's not surprising if you haven't. Often we're so driven to compete and win that we don't actually get to this way of communicating.

Think about your own experiences with conflict resolution. Can you come up with an example of a win/lose strategy and a lose/lose strategy? How could they have been done differently to arrive at a win/win situation?

It's important to learn from the past. It's not that we want to dwell on past situations, but by pointing out what could have been done and what was done well, we can do better moving forward.

Chapter 6: What's Your Conflict Style?

Before you can improve your conflict style, you need to understand it. In this chapter you'll be offered a quiz to determine your own conflict style as well as how to interpret your results.

It's important that you be as realistic and honest as possible. Of course, we always want our answers to make us "look good" but you don't have to show this to anyone else. Only by becoming aware of your own attitudes and behaviors can you make important changes that move you forward.

Conflict Resolution Style Questionnaire

Circle or record the answer that best reflects your truth.

1. I am usually firm in pursuing my goals?

   Very Unlikely   Unlikely   Likely   Very Likely

2. I try to win my position.

   Very Unlikely   Unlikely   Likely   Very Likely

3. I give up on some points in exchange for others.

   Very Unlikely   Unlikely   Likely   Very Likely

4. I feel that differences are not always worth worrying about.

   Very Unlikely   Unlikely   Likely   Very Likely

5. I try to find a position that is intermediate between his/her and mine.

   Very Unlikely   Unlikely   Likely   Very Likely

6. In approaching negotiations, I try to be considerate of the other person's wishes.

   Very Unlikely   Unlikely   Likely   Very Likely

7. I try to show the logic and benefits of my positions.

   Very Unlikely   Unlikely   Likely   Very Likely

8. I always lean toward a direct discussion of the problem.

   Very Unlikely   Unlikely   Likely   Very Likely

9. I try to find a fair combination of gains and losses for both of us.

   Very Unlikely   Unlikely   Likely   Very Likely

10. I attempt to immediately work through our differences.

    Very Unlikely   Unlikely   Likely   Very Likely

11. I try to avoid creating unpleasantness for myself.

    Very Unlikely   Unlikely   Likely   Very Likely

12. I might try to soothe the other's feelings and preserve our friendship.

    Very Unlikely   Unlikely   Likely   Very Likely

13. I attempt to get all concerns and issues immediately out in the open.

Very Unlikely   Unlikely   Likely   Very Likely

14. I sometimes avoid taking positions that would create controversy.

Very Unlikely   Unlikely   Likely   Very Likely

15. I try not to hurt other's feelings.

Very Unlikely   Unlikely   Likely   Very Likely

Scoring the Questionnaire

In order to score the answers to your questions, assign the following points:

Very likely – 1 point, Unlikely – 2 points, Likely – 3 points, Very Likely – 4 points

Now you'll need to get more specific to arrange your answers by type of conflict management style. Add up the points for each of the following categories as follows:

Authoritative/Competitive – Add Items 1, 2, and 8 for a total of

_____

Problem Solving – Add Items 8, 10, and 13 for a total of

_____

Compromising – Add items 3, 5, and 9 for a total of

_____

Avoiding – Add items 4, 11, and 14 for a total of

_____

Smoothing – Add items 6, 12, and 15 for a total of

_____

Interpreting your Answers

The areas where you score the highest show that you have higher concerns in those areas. Those most closely match your own personal conflict style. The lowest numbers are the least likely to be your conflict style.

Let's take a look at each type of style in more depth so you can understand what this says about the way you handle conflict.

Smoothing.

If you scored high in the area of smoothing, you have high concern for other people. You usually try to smooth over disagreements or you ignore them so that you can avoid conflict. This helps to keep things peaceful on the surface, but often conflict will rise again.

There are some pros to this type of conflict management. For example:

- It's diplomatic and other people appreciate it

- You give a lot of compliments and help people feel good about themselves

- It can create an opportunity to have discussions in the future while avoiding tension

But smoothing also has some negative aspects including:

- This style doesn't help you to find an actual resolution to the conflict

- It takes longer to get to a resolution and the conflict often returns to the surface causing more problems

There are times when the smoothing style can serve you well. For example, it can allow someone else to be heard, to learn and it shows that you're a reasonable person.

Smoothing is also something you can use when you don't care as much about the issue as someone else does – you can let it go easily.

Smoothing also satisfies others and in the short-term can help you to have more cooperation. This might open the door to working on conflict issues later. You can also earn high favor from others which will serve you later if you need their grace.

If you're in a situation where it's important to have stability and peace, smoothing can also work in your favor. Overall, this style only works for the short-term, though. It doesn't actually solve problems.

Avoidance.

Avoidance is a style where you seek to stay neutral. Unlike smoothing, this type of conflict resolution style has less concern for others and more concern for self. This style is more likely to cause you to isolate yourself and try not to have to actually deal with the situation.

There are some advantages for you personally with this style such as:

- You don't have to work hard at communicating

- It's the easy road

But there are also problems with this style such as:

- When this style is used often it can lead to resentment from unresolved issues

- This system can be difficult on your self-esteem – you don't empower yourself to deal with problems

Avoidance is okay to use in some situations. For example, if a conflict is really trivial and doesn't matter in the scheme of things it might be okay to avoid it in favor of working on other issues.

Avoidance also gets used when you feel like you don't have a chance of really getting what you want. This is also a style that can be used at times when you feel that the disruption of dealing with the conflict will cause more problems than it will solve.

This may also be a useful style when you need to take a break and allow people to cool down from a disagreement. Finally, it might be okay to use avoidance when there are others you feel could do a better job of resolving the conflict positively.

While there can be a few advantages to avoidance, the bottom line is that this style of conflict doesn't actually resolve anything. While it might push an issue onto the backburner for a little while, it will only come back again.

Compromise.

Compromise means bargaining and looking to find middle ground. This is often what people consider to be a victory, but really no one gets what they really wanted and everyone must sacrifice something.

While this can give you a solution that will work, it doesn't really give you the best of all possibilities. Compromise has benefits such as:

- It can help move toward a resolution when it's used as part of negotiation tactics

- It can help to break a deadlock where neither party is working toward ending the conflict

But with compromise, there is a downside. Some of the problems include:

- Nobody is really satisfied – everyone had to give up a piece of what they really wanted

- This doesn't always lead to an actual resolution – often the issues resurface

- Sometimes compromising can make you feel like you sold out instead of fighting for what you really wanted

Compromising is a common conflict style and it can be useful at times. It can work if you have goals that really matter to you, but they're not worth the effort at the time to fight harder for them. The outcome won't improve the situation enough so you find it better to sacrifice some of your wants.

You may also need to compromise when your conflict is with someone who is as equal in power or even more powerful and is seeking goals that are mutually exclusive to yours.

Compromise can also give you a temporary solution that gives you time to go back to problem solving at a later time. You may also need to use compromise if you're in a situation where time is an issue. It may be faster to compromise than to truly resolve the conflict.

Authoritative Command.

Authoritative command is a conflict resolution style that works if you hold the power. This is when conflict is suppressed by allowing a boss or third party make the decision without compromising. This usually leads to win-lose power struggles.

Authoritative command work in some ways including:

- It can be a good short-term resolution to allow people to cool off and come back to the table

- It's a good style for emergencies when it's not possible to spend more time solving problems

- It can make you feel powerful if you're the one in control

There can be negative aspects to this approach as well including:

- This approach can make you feared or unpopular with your employees – especially if you use it often

- This doesn't give you anywhere to go if you put your foot down, but there still isn't a resolution

This technique is one that should be used judiciously, but it can be helpful in some cases. For example, this is an appropriate technique to use in an emergency where time is a constraint.

This can also be used on important issues when you're forced to make bottom line decisions such as cutting costs and enforcing unpopular but necessary rules. This can also be needed when you're making decisions that are critical to the life of your company and you know that you're right about the choice you need to make.

Problem Solving.

The problem solving approach is one that often takes longer, but takes more factors into consideration. It takes into account all the facts, emotions, doubts, and reservations of all parties involved. The process allows you to work through all the issues.

Problem solving is generally the best way to deal with conflict resolution if you want long-term results. It can:

- Help all parties to keep an open mind

- Move all parties to a resolution that's satisfactory

- Helps everyone feel that they're being heard and can meet important goals

There are some cons to this approach, even though it's generally the best way to go. For example:

- This process takes time and may not work in an emergency – however you can come back to this once a crisis is averted to worth through the issues

- It's not always worth the effort especially if the payoff isn't very valuable and doesn't have a long-term impact

There are many reasons why using a problem solving style can be very beneficial. This is a great process that will help you find solutions that help everyone with concerns to feel heard and keeps people from having to compromise on important issues.

Problem solving really helps if your objective is to learn and understand all parties concerned. And you can benefit from the insights that come from people with different perspectives. This can be a very constructive process that opens you up to new ideas.

When you perform conflict resolution with problem solving you'll be more likely to have buy-in from everyone involved which leads to better productivity. You also allow people to work through feelings that have kept conflict fueled.

Reflecting On Your Conflict Style

Now that you've looked at how you scored and the pros and cons of each of these conflict management styles, consider how your conflict style has served you. Chances are you've had trouble with conflict in the past.

Does your new understanding make it clear why conflict has been difficult for you in the past? What can you change about your conflict style that will help you move toward more positive, healthy relationships and communication?

It's important to be really aware of your strengths and also the areas where you can improve your skill set. Most people have to learn skills that help them to communicate better – it usually doesn't come innately.

And many people have had poor examples of conflict resolution and really don't know the best way to go about it. But, like any other skill, you can make improvements and work to get better at this type of communication.

Chapter 7: Using Positive Communication to Resolve Conflict

It's really important to use positive communication skills when you're trying to resolve a conflict of any kind. But many people aren't familiar with the steps that are needed to implement that type of communication.

In this chapter we'll discuss the role of communication in conflict resolution and share some skills that will help you to make improvements.

The Communication Funnel

Because we have different perspectives and biases, we don't always hear what a speaker is really trying to say. It's important to understand some of the barriers to hearing the information that's being given in the most objective way.

One model that helps you to look at this is the communication funnel. This is the idea that what you hear in broad terms gets narrowed down by your own perceptions and other barriers.

Barriers Related to the Speaker

First we begin with the speaker. When you listen to someone speak, you don't just hear their words. There are many factors involved in addition to the words they say such as their expressions, tone of voice, and body language.

All of these issues can color what you hear. When you're speaking, you need to keep these factors in mind. Let's look at each one in more depth.

Your Words.

A speaker's words can be very powerful. But some of the things you might be tempted to say can get in the way of your message.

Be careful not to speak in absolutes such as saying things like "always" and "never". Rarely do those words accurately describe a situation.

Using the word "but" too often can also cause a negative effect. You may contradict yourself too often. You should also avoid using complex words and jargon that might not be clearly understood. This can turn a listener off and keep them from hearing your message.

When you use negative words such as "can't" or "won't" you give the listener the impression that you're not willing to compromise or listen to their side of things – even if that's not true for you. It's always best to use positive words that bring a positive perception to the listener.

Facial Expressions.

Non-verbal messages can be as important as the actual words you say. Your face is the most important of all the non-verbal cues that you give to your listeners. If your face looks angry or disinterested, you'll lose your audience.

You should also avoid expressions that could seem offensive such as:

- Eye rolling

- Frowning

- Avoiding eye-contact

- Frowning

While there are some cultures that find eye contact offensive, the majority of people do appreciate it. Make sure to know your audience. Overall you want to look pleasant, alert, interested, and relaxed as you speak to someone.

Tone of Voice.

Tone of voice can also cause your listener to hear different things. If your voice is monotone or too soft you may lose the interest of the listener. Some other qualities to avoid include:

- Speaking too loudly

- Using a sarcastic tone

- Speaking too fast

- Speaking too slowly

- Sounding impatient

- Unclear speech

All of these can cause problems in their own ways. You want to have the goal of speaking loudly enough that your audience can hear you, but not so loud that you give them a headache.

You should also speak slowly enough that your words are clear. It's also good to use dynamics when you speak – sometimes getting louder and getting softer when appropriate as well as changing the pitch of your voice so that it isn't monotone.

When you sound sincere and truly interested in the subject of which you speak, the listener will naturally become more interested in what you have to say and is more likely to hear you in an objective way.

Body Language.

Facial expressions are important, but there are other types of body language that are also critical. You also need to think about the way that you hold yourself when you're speaking.

For example, if you spend time shifting in your chair, rifling through papers, or looking at your watch you seem uninterested in the conversation. You should also avoid crossing your arms as that can be an aggressive stance.

Crossing your arms may be interpreted as disinterested or being adversarial – even if you don't feel that way. Try, instead, to keep your arms relaxed at your sides and also work to lean toward the person you're speaking to and listening to.

The Listener's Barriers

Now that we've looked at some of the things a speaker can do that lead to communication barriers it's important to understand how the listener can also funnel information through their own barriers.

A listener might make judgments based on their own experiences and knowledge. These may have nothing to do with the speaker, but still cause what the speaker is saying to be misinterpreted or unheard.

Education.

Education can cause problems when it comes to communication. For example, if the speaker has an education in a specific area and uses complicated terms and jargon the listener may just turn off when they don't understand.

But someone who has the same education in specific area may be riveted by the exact same conversation. It's important to know your audience and make sure that you're on the same page. Trying to make sure you're on even footing is helpful.

Assumptions.

It's not uncommon for people to make assumptions about people that really don't have anything to do with the facts about that person. You may misinterpret something a speaker says, body language, or facial expressions that get in the way of positive communication.

Emotional State.

Have you ever been to a movie when you were in a bad mood and disliked it? But maybe you watched it a few months later when it came out on DVD and found it to be wonderful? Your emotional state has a lot to do with the way you feel in any given situation.

If you're upset – even if it's about something else – you can disengage from a speaker or stop listening.

Distractions.

There are often distractions when you're working toward active listening. This could be phone calls, text messages, or interruptions by other people. You may also be distracted by something going on at home such as a sick child or financial stress. Any or all of these factors can keep you from really hearing what someone else is saying.

Interpreting Meaning.

When you add up all of these factors, it's no wonder that miscommunication is a common problem. One way that you can eliminate some of the problems that go along with misinterpreting meaning is to be an active listener.

Active Listening

Active listening is the idea that as the listener you have just as much responsibility in the conversation as the speaker. You're not just passively listening as the words go by.

Instead, you're trying to grasp what the speaker is saying – the facts they're sharing as well as their feelings and opinions.

With active listening, it's important that you actually show respect to the speaker and value his or her point of view. You're not worried about what you're going to say in response, you're simply giving all your attention to the speaker's words.

This type of listening breeds trust – something that's essential for conflict resolution and healthy communication.

How Listening Helps

Listening is a huge part of communication. You may have heard the expression that you have two ears and one mouth for a reason. Often we're more concerned about what we say than how we listen. But really, the opposite is necessary if you want to have positive interactions.

Active listening can help to bring about true change. It's the most important part of changes in personality, developing a group, and resolving conflict. Listening can change the way people think about themselves and others.

If you're listened to you become:

- More emotionally mature

- More democratic

- Less defensive

- Less authoritarian

Listen actually helps you to choose your own words carefully and express your own meaning more clearly. In a group, listening helps reduce problems with arguments. People feel freer to give their opinions and share their thoughts without the fear of criticism.

Listening helps people to have more information, build positive relationships with one another, and helps everyone to have a more positive attitude. It lends itself to constructive changes and helps everyone to grow.

How to Listen Actively

Listening may seem like second nature, but as you get older and experience so many distractions as well as negative experiences, listening actually becomes a lost art. But when you practice active listening you can experience real change in yourself and in those around you.

Often you develop a picture of yourself that comes from experiences you have and the way you think and feel about yourself. In the past, listening to others may be difficult if what they're saying doesn't fit our own mental picture.

But with active listening, you don't worry about the threat to your own mental picture. Instead, you remain open. You can explore what someone else is pointing out to you make your own decisions about the validity of what they're saying without it threatening your confidence and self-worth.

When you're willing to be open to others' ideas and them to yours, you can experience change. This promotes freedom and equality between people. It helps to shape understanding in positive ways and leads to acceptance.

When you develop a safe place for listening and sharing ideas, people feel comfortable and can let down their guard. With this safe space, new experiences and changes in values can take place. This allows everyone to express their own truth and feel good about their views as well as becoming open to changing those views.

This is Not Active Listening

Active listening is peaceful, natural, warm, and safe. There are many elements that can harm the ability to embrace active listening. The following actions can destroy the trust you've developed:

- Pleading with someone to change their mind

- Scolding someone for their beliefs or opinions

- Prodding your conversation partner to get more information

- Insulting another in order to persuade them in a different direction

- Demanding someone make a decision

- Judging another's experiences or opinions

It can be hard for you to be open to listening to someone else's view especially if it's very far away from your own. The idea of active listening isn't to change anyone's opinions. It's simply to understand their point of view.

The more open your mind is, the more active listening will become and the more successful your communication will be. If someone puts you on the spot and demands you make a decision, you can acknowledge the question without answering and compromising your own needs.

For example, if someone might ask you a question such as: Don't you think that I'm doing a better job than my coworker?

You don't have to answer this question directly or make a judgment. Instead, you can reflect on what you hear them saying. A good answer would be: It sounds like you feel that you're really doing a good job.

This doesn't put anyone down or dismiss the opinion of the person with whom you're speaking. Instead, it shows that you've been listening actively without making any assumptions or judgments.

This allows you to leave the door open so that the other person can share more about what they're feeling. As they unpack their statements, you'll gain better understanding of the issues. You'll be helping to think with a person, but not think for them or make judgments about them.

You should avoid giving advice whenever possible – especially if you're not asked for it. This often is seen as a way to change a person rather than a way to really be helpful. Giving advice can keep someone from sharing how they really feel.

Techniques for Active Listening

Now that you understand how important active listening is, you're ready for some concrete strategies to help you improve this skill. It really is a skill that anyone can learn and implement in his or her life.

It may require some practice and you'll make mistakes, but over time you'll find that you get better and better at active listening. As you do, you'll see your relationships improve and you'll have fewer problems with conflict. You may have different points of view, but it will be easier to solve issues before they escalate.

Listen for Total Meaning.

Almost every message delivered by a person has two parts – the content itself and an underlying feeling. When you listen you want to try to get both messages.

Listen for clues that help you to understand more than just the words that are being spoken. For example, a coworker may say to you, "I finished the report." This is a message that the report is finished and could even indicate they could add a new task.

But if someone at the end of a long day says, "I've finally finished this tedious report!" You can also interpret that they have worked hard and have had enough for the day. If you were to ask them to do something else in this moment, you might not get a very helpful response.

While both statements tell you that the report is done, they don't express the same total meaning. Being sensitive to the entire meaning being conveyed can help you to respond in ways that validate your coworker and foster a positive relationship.

For example, when responding to the second version of the message you might say, "That sounds like it was hard work. Glad to have it completed?" and if you have something else you need done a good response might be, "Do you feel like working on anything else after that?"

This response tells your coworker that you've heard what they've said and meant and that you understand it was hard work. Asking before assigning another project shows respect.

Feelings vs. Content.

When a person makes a statement it may be more important to respond to the feelings they're sharing rather than the content of what they said. For example, if a coworker says, "I'm so sick of this computer I'd like to throw it out the window," you don't really need to respond to the content.

It's obvious they're having computer problems, but that they aren't actually going to throw the computer. Instead, respond to the feelings behind the statement.

For example, "Wow, sounds like you're really frustrated." This shows that you are paying attention to the other's feelings and helps to improve trust.

Pay Attention to All Cues.

We've already discussed that not all communication is verbal. Pay attention to those nonverbal cues that give you an idea of the feelings underneath the content.

Look for the inflections, facial expressions, and body language that make up the message.

Paraphrasing.

One way that you can show the speaker that you're listening actively is to paraphrase what they're saying to you. In other words, you'll use your own words to say what you think the speaker said.

You might begin your paraphrasing efforts with opening statements like:

- It sounds like you're saying…

- This is what I'm hearing you say…

- Let me make sure I understand you…

After you've completed your paraphrase, check back with the speaker to see if you're correct. You can ask, "Did I get that right?"

This gives the speaker the opportunity to make any corrections or agree that you've understood him well.

This type of paraphrasing works well in communication because it has a calming effect on the speaker. It communicates to the speaker that what he's saying to you is important.

Sometimes when someone is speaking you may feel confused about what they're saying. Paraphrasing also gives you the chance to make sure that you really do understand what's being said. It can also help the speaker to get clarity about their own point of view.

Paraphrasing also gives the speaker to hear their own point of view out loud. This can either reassure him he's on the right track or can give him pause and help him to rethink his position.

In any case, this is a wonderful way to support active listening and foster trust and communication. You're not using any judgment, only understanding.

Asking Powerful Questions.

Questions are another way to ramp up your listening skills. Asking questions can help you to get more information, get clarity, and help you lead your conversation partner to see things in a new way.

There are two types of questions – open and closed. Open questions help to open up the conversation because they require a more descriptive response. Closed questions, on the other hand, can be answered with a simple yes or no that ends the dialogue.

You want to use as many open questions as possible when you practice active listening. Here are a few helpful questions that can get you started. The more you use open questions, the easier it will be to come up with your own.

- What do you think about….?

- Would it be helpful if I…?

- What do you think we can do about this?

- Help me understand where you're coming from on this…

- What would you like me to stop doing?

- What would you like me to do more often?

- I'm prepared to…Would that ease the…?

- Let's set a time when we can get back together and talk about what changes we're both prepared to make.

- How can I help make this situation better?

Remember that when you ask these types of questions, you need to be sincerely seeking answers. If you're asking great questions, but throwing out negative nonverbal messages the conversation won't go anywhere.

Nonverbal Cues.

It's important to remember the nonverbal cues we've already discussed such as eye contact, attention, positive facial expressions, and a good tone of voice. These are all essential pieces of the active listening puzzle.

Active Listening Can Be Difficult.

Active listening isn't easy. It may require you to retrain everything about the way you communicate with other people. But the results are worth the effort. Some things that make it difficult to listen actively include:

- It requires us to be sincerely interested

- We have to be willing to risk changing our own feelings and opinions

- Active listening means we sometimes have to hear negative feelings and even hostile language

- We will sometimes feel uncomfortable

- We have to accept that our own ideas may be challenged

- We're required to set aside our own concerns and control our emotions as we listen to the feelings of others

If you can push through these difficulties you'll have more success with active listening. This will be one of the most important steps you can take toward healthy conflict resolution.

Evaluating Your Communication Skills

Now that we've discussed some of the most important aspects of communication, it's time to reflect on your own skills.

- In which areas are you strong?

- What areas require some more work on your part?

- How have you seen the communication funnel work in your own experience?

- What difference would active listening make in you relationships?

As you consider your communication skills and are really honest with yourself, you'll be able to make positive changes that foster healthy and happy relationships in the workplace as well as in your personal relationships.

Chapter 8: There's More Than One Way to Resolve Conflict

When it comes to resolving conflict there's more than one way to be successful. It helps to have many different strategies in your toolbox so that you can approach every situation confidently.

In this chapter we'll look at a variety of strategies that can help you to resolve conflict and improve communication and results.

Seven Step Solution

The Seven Step Solution is one way that you can work to resolve conflict. This is a great guideline to use for quick results and success. Take a look at each step and consider how you can make this work in your environment.

1. Be sincere.

You must be willing to remove all masks and speak with sincerity. You really have to want to work things out in order to solve problems.

2. Identify the problem.

Sometimes the things that people are discussing aren't really the problem. Someone might be complaining about her schedule, but in reality the problem comes with the frustration from feeling that she's doing more than her fair share. Uncovering the hidden problem is critical.

3. Listen first so you can be received.

The first step toward conflict resolution involves being a good listener. When you listen and make sure to clarify what you understand, the other party will be more inclined to hear your point of view and really listen to you.

4. Don't play to win.

Often in a conflict, it becomes more about winning and being right than solving the problem. The best conflict resolution occurs when you give up the idea that you have to win and instead really look for a way to make everyone happy.

When you try to be right and fight for your position, you actually cause more conflict and build walls instead of bridges.

5. Come up with several solutions.

Most of the time there's more than one way to resolve a problem. Take the time to consider several possibilities. This gives you more opportunities to create a solution that everyone can agree on.

6. Evaluate options and choose one.

For every solution you develop, take the time to evaluate it. Come up with a list of pros and cons. Evaluate what you think will work best.

Look at which option gives both sides what they want and which ones will be most sustainable. Then select the one that works best. If possible, don't rush your decision.

7. Focus on the value of the relationship.

The point of positive conflict resolution is to preserve the relationship. With that as your focus, you can have a better chance of maintain a healthy relationship.

The Conflict/Opportunity Test

The Conflict/Opportunity Test is another way that you can work to solve a conflict. This consists of asking yourself a series of questions to determine what the actual conflict is and what the benefits are of resolving it in a variety of ways.

Some questions you can ask yourself include:

- What is the conflict?

- Who is involved in this conflict?

- If the conflict is resolved, what are the benefits?

- If the conflict isn't resolved, will I have any benefits or payoffs?

- If the conflict is not resolved, will there be any harm to any party?

- If the conflict is resolved, will the situation become better than it was before the conflict occurred?

- Whatever the outcome, can I see that the conflict was constructive and added to a more positive outcome?

Evaluating conflict in this way can help you decide how to deal with it. If resolving the conflict won't actually improve anything, it's possible that it's not as big of a problem as you thought.

If you see that the conflict could really bring about important change, it's worth pursuing positive conflict resolution measures.

Visualizing Conflict

If you're a very visual person, as many are, it can help to visualize the conflict in a chart or map. In this way you can get a better idea of the key players, the problems and improve the likelihood of reaching a solution.

Conflict Resolution Needs/Goals.

With this type of visualization, you'll look at each player in the conflict and what they need. You can create a chart as follows to help get the most important facts:

Conflict	
Person 1	Person 2
Stated Position	Stated Position
Needs	Needs
Assumptions	Assumptions

Each person in the conflict has a specific position that's driven by his or her needs. And needs are driven by assumptions about how they can be filled, about what's possible and what isn't, and about how the world works.

Assumptions can be made from opinions, beliefs, or facts. It's important that you really understand the underlying issues.

Filling out this diagram can help you to get clarity about what's going on. It also gives everyone a chance to make sure that they're being represented correctly.

Charting Conflict Resolution Phases.

You may also want to use a chart that walks you step by step through the process of conflict resolution. A simple two column chart will give you great clarity.

In the first column you'll write down the phases and in the second column you can write down the results of each step. There are five steps you'll find helpful in creating this particular chart.

1. Identify the Problem.

 For this step you'll want to write down a statement of the overall problem. To do this you'll need to use active listening techniques and write down the other person's statement on a post-it note. Then you'll switch roles and the other person will write down your statement on a post-it note.

From here you can determine which areas you agree upon and clarify the areas where you disagree.

2. Identify the Common Goal.

As you discuss the issue, is there a common goal that you can both agree to? Usually there is some area where you can find common ground. You'll need to continue discussions until you can find at least one area where you can reach an agreement.

3. Identify and Rate the Underlying Needs.

Talk with the other party about what they need and write down what you discover on a post it note. Then have the person rate their needs from 1-10. Switch roles and allow the other party to identify your needs and then rank them yourself.

Look to see if you have any common needs. At this point you can begin to see some possible win/win solutions. Make sure that everyone has a clear understanding of all parties' needs.

4. Explore Assumptions.

It's important to get clear about the assumptions everyone brings to the table. Take the time to brainstorm some assumptions that each person has. Offer assumptions from the other person.

At this point you can also challenge some of the assumptions you discover using facts. Look at all the assumptions and see if there are any themes across the board. Again check to see if there is a win/win solution.

5. Brainstorm Solution.

At this point you'll understand more about each other's positions. This is a good time to brainstorm potential solutions. If you've used active listening and developed a trusting conversation, you'll be able to throw out many ideas without worrying about criticism.

Check each brainstorm against the most important needs of each party. Then choose a solution that works best and develop a plan for implementing it. You may even want to schedule a time to come back to the discussion and see if anything needs to be tweaked.

Following this strategy using sticky notes and large paper can help you to visualize the conflict and can help everyone to get on the same page.

A Colorful Conflict Resolution Strategy.

Color can be a wonderful way to visualize a conflict and stimulate the brain to come up with creative solutions. Color is used by many project managers to help spark ideas and solutions.

With this strategy there are five phases of conflict resolution that can be used. You'll use different colors to help organize your thoughts and develop solutions.

You'll need post-it notes, flipchart paper, and five different colored markers.

Color 1 Phase One: Identify the Problem.

First, tape a flipchart paper to the wall or use a flipchart on an easel. Write down the overall problem on a post it note. Place it on the flipchart.

Have the first person give his or her stated position. At this time there is no need to give reasons for the position. It's only important to state it.

The other person should practice active listening and when he or she really understand the problem from the other person's point of view, the listener should write it on a post-it note and place it below the conflict statement.

Now you should switch roles and repeat this step. At this point, you should identify areas where you can agree. Write these areas on post-it notes and place them between the two positions.

Is there an obvious solution already forming? If so, the conflict is resolved and you have no need of moving to the next phase.

If you have areas of disagreement, you should also write them down on post-it notes and place them on the flipchart.

Color 2 Phase Two: Identify the Common Goal.

As you move to this phase, you'll write with a different colored marker. You'll need to define a common goal that both of you share. This should be something that's more important than the conflict you're experiencing.

Write that goal on a post-it note and place it on the top of the chart above the problem statement from Phase One. Now ask a few questions to make sure you're on the right track such as:

- Is the conflict defined specifically enough or is it too broad?

- Is the conflict defined in too narrow of a way?

- Is there an obvious solution?

If there's an obvious solution, the conflict is resolved. Other questions to ask include:

- Does each person or party feel heard?

- Does each person feel his or her position is being taken seriously?

Color 3 Phase Three: Identify and Rate Underlying Needs.

For this phase person 1 should ask person 2 what his or her needs are and record them on a post-it note. This should be placed beneath the stated problem.

Then person 2 should rate his needs using a scale from 1-10 with 10 being the highest level of need. Afterwards, you should switch roles and person 2 should ask person 1 about needs.

At this point, identify any needs you have in common. Write these between the two columns of post-it notes that you've been building. Again, test if there is a possible win/win solution.

Complete another check to make sure that the conflict is defined properly. The more you discuss a situation, the clearer the real conflict can become.

You may discover that there was a hidden problem that is the real issue. Make sure that every party feels heard and understood.

Color 4 Phase Four: Explore Assumptions.

At this point you should brainstorm the assumptions that are driving each other's needs. You don't need to challenge any of the ideas, just write them down.

Each person should have the opportunity to offer up any assumptions that he thinks the other person may hold. You can add these only if both parties agree.

If there are facts that can challenge assumptions, discuss them. You can only change the post-it note if the other person agrees.

Are there any themes in the assumptions? If so, write those down on post-it notes. At this point check to see if there is a possible win/win solution.

Again, check the process to make sure the information on the paper is accurate and that everyone feels heard and validated.

Color 5 Phase Five: Brainstorm Solutions.

At this point it's time to turn the focus on solutions. Together you can brainstorm possible solutions. Give each idea its own post-it note and use no judgment at this point.

Check the brainstormed solutions against common goals and each person's most important needs. Then choose a solution. Make sure that the solution meets the highest needs of both parties.

Then develop an implementation plan for the solution. It's also a good idea to make sure and leave the conversation open.

You can always come back to the table and discuss how the solution is going. Is it really meeting the most important needs? If not, you can tweak it as needed.

If at any point during the process you come up with an acceptable solution, you can suspend the activity and stop at that phase. But if you're struggling to come up with a solution, the five phases can give you ample opportunity.

Seeing all the information laid out in a colorful array can help you to visualize the issues and make important choices.

Facilitating Conflict

As you learn better and better conflict resolution skills you may find yourself in the role of facilitator. You might be mediating between two people or you may be facilitating the conflict of two groups. This position can be intimidating, but when you have the right skills you can handle it.

Why Facilitate? Often people in leadership positions aren't equipped to handle conflict. You're probably experienced a leader who ignored resistance and forced people to submit to their will without hearing criticism.

Using this kind of force with people on your team reduces their trust in you. They may comply because they need to keep their income, but that doesn't mean they'll be happy about it or be their most productive.

This approach makes people feel less valued and reduces their trust in you. People and groups will often start looking for another place to work where they feel their thoughts and opinions are valued.

And if you're not the person who has power over control of a group, it's impossible to force your will on a group you're leading. Instead of trying to control, it makes more sense to understand and make decisions together.

Confrontational Facilitation.

As you lead a group, you may find that people are behaving in a polite manner rather than really sharing their thoughts and ideas. You don't always have to be confrontational as a facilitator, but if people aren't being open and honest you may have to push for information.

At first people may be intimidated and not really want to leave their comfort zone, but doing so makes everything work better. Sometimes people will even ask to be pushed out of their comfort zone and deal with problems by saying, "We need to face our problems." If you don't take advantage, you'll miss out on important information.

In order to progress to this type of facilitation, it's important that you've had experience with conflict resolution and can handle any type of conflict that arises as part of an open discussion.

For everyone to feel that they can speak openly, you'll have to set norms that make it possible for people to share their ideas without feeling criticized. You'll need to give everyone boundaries and guidelines to follow.

Managing Differences in a Collaborative Way.

There are some behaviors that help to manage differences while others keep people from being able to speak freely and create constructive solutions.

As a facilitator, you need to be the best example of appropriate behaviors including:

- Letting people vent – they need to feel they can be open and honest and after venting, people can begin problem solving

- Asking for differing views

- Paraphrasing to show active listening

- Respecting opposing views

- Making eye contact and using body language that communicates openness

- Staying calm and avoiding defensiveness

- Validating speakers

- Redirecting those using sarcasm or criticism

- Confronting facts

- Taking a problem-solving approach

- Using norms for control (we'll discuss norms more in the next chapter)

- Showing appreciation and concern for feelings

- Checking on people to see how they're doing

- Disclosing personal feelings

- Bringing closure to the solution

- Making sure everyone is involved – drawing out those who might be quiet

- Evaluating how the team did during the conflict to help learn from mistakes and celebrate victories

These behaviors will help you to lead by example and stay in control of the situation. It will allow people to feel free to discuss their feelings and give you the input that helps lead to a solution.

Of course there are also some negative behaviors that will get in the way of your progress. You need to make sure you avoid these actions that can hinder the discussion.

- Arguing

- Defensiveness

- Entrapping people with pointed questions

- Allowing a few individuals to dominate the discussion

- Favoring any side of the debate

- Letting the discussion turn overly emotional or personal

- Ending the discussion before a resolution has been established

- Avoiding hot button issues

- Having no process or plan in mind

- Not using norms

- Lacking empathy for the feelings of others

- Allowing a discussion to drag on with no real progress

Before approaching conflict resolution facilitation, it's important to be prepared. You need to be ready to handle a difficult situation. That also means you need to be aware of what can trigger your own anger and avoid that trap.

You can prepare by gathering as much information as possible about the issue and about the people or groups you'll be facilitating. Trying to have empathy and understand the different perspectives will serve you well.

It's important that you are sincere and caring with people so that they can open up to you. You also need to make sure you don't take yourself too seriously as you facilitate a group. Don't allow the issues to become about you personally.

Healthy vs. Dysfunctional Debates.

In a healthy debate people will be open to hearing each other's ideas. They'll listen and respond to ideas whether or not they agree with them. There will be an attitude of trying to understand.

In a healthy debate people are objective and they focus on facts rather than personalities. In addition, there's a system in place to analyze the situation and problem solve.

In a dysfunctional argument, you have very different dynamics. People may assume they're right without being open to others' ideas. In this setting, there's little regard for understanding how other people see a situation.

With dysfunctional arguments people make arguments personal and use blaming. There's also little structure to allow problem solving to take place.

You can work to make debates healthier with a variety of techniques including:

- Staying totally neutral with your own position

- Pointing out differences in an effort to understand

- Remind people and insist that they listen politely by referring to ground rules

- Push people to paraphrase each other's' ideas to promote understanding

- Ask people to share their concerns

- Bring the focus back to the facts

- Invite feedback and be ready to accept feedback about yourself

- Be assertive in your facilitation

- Get closure and move forward on specific issues

By using these techniques you can promote a healthy debate. You want to avoid behaviors such as joining the argument and ignoring differences. You also need to make sure you don't allow people to become rude and stop listening to each other.

In addition, you can't allow hot button issues to be sidestepped – conflict resolution is about getting everything out in the open. You mustn't let people get personal or defense. And you must actively participate in making the debate healthy.

Two Steps of Facilitation.

There are two steps to facilitating conflict in a positive way. The first is venting. Venting allows people to get their emotions out in the open.

Many people hold back about their feelings and this keeps them from being able to problem solve. You need to allow people to share their feelings first.

You can facilitate this step by:

- Slowing down the discussion so you can take notes and listen actively

- Staying completely neutral in the words you say as well as your body language

- Staying calm

- Going back to the norms and ground rules

- Behaving assertively and maintain control over the group insisting that people speak one at a time and being actively involved

- Explaining the difference between a debate and an argument

- Intervening when people make things personal or become rude

- Emphasizing listening and being a good example

- Calling for a break when things become too intense

- Using a flip chart to create a visual display

- Create closure by asking the group to summarize agreements

The second step is actually resolving the issue. Once people have had the opportunity to vent, you can more onto a more structured approach that helps to get solutions. It's important to facilitate a collaborative process.

You need to identify the issues and keep people engaged in analyzing the conflict, generating creative ideas, and looking at a wide variety of potential solutions. Before trying to come up with a solution, you'll really explore all the issues.

Solutions are generated by a process that accepts all ideas and eliminates competition and power. At the end of the discussion, everyone should feel heard and that he or she was a part of the final solution.

While this method does take more time, it's the best way to make sure that everyone feels satisfied with the solution at the end.

Chapter 9: Keeping Conflict at Bay

When you need to have an important meeting or discussion, it's important that you set norms. These are guidelines that help everyone to stay on their best behavior and keep the conversation healthy.

Creating Norms

Allowing the members of the group to help create the norms will allow them to buy in to them. You can use questions to help create the norms for your group such as:

- What rules and behaviors can we agree on when we find that we have disagreements?

- What can we do to make sure our debates are healthy and productive rather than becoming an argument?

- Some norms that make sense for conflict resolution include:

- Speaking one at a time

- Looking at the person who is speaking and acknowledging valid points

- Accepting all ideas as valid

- Building on each other's ideas

- Exploring every idea that's presented

- Allowing everyone in the group to be heard – not just a few vocal people

- Avoiding getting overly emotional, personal, or argumentative

- No one will attack anyone else

- We will call a time out if the discussion gets too heated

- No one will deliberately cause a problem

- We'll look at fixing the system rather than coming from a place of personal points of view

As you discuss the norms for your group, you need to write them down on a flipchart so that people can review them and be reminded of appropriate behaviors that you've all agreed to.

You may need to add new ground rules as the discussion continues and difficulties arise. You should also feel that you can go back and refer to the norms in an assertive way when people go off course. And you can expect that people will go off course.

Check In

When it's time for a break, survey the group and allow them to assess how the session is going. You'll have them answer on a scale from 1-5, with 1 being definitely not and 5 being absolutely.

Have the group reflect on statement such as:

- We are really making meaningful progress

- We are dealing with the right issues

- We are being honest and open

- Our solutions will make improvements

Creating a quick questionnaire helps the group to evaluate their own behavior and progress and allows them to come back from a break with fresh eyes. It can also help you as a facilitator to see how they're feeling about the process.

When to Intervene

If, during the discussion, you can sense that a major problem is brewing you'll need to intervene. This can happen when someone isn't listening, people are having side conversations, comments are getting personal, or the discussion has gone off the rails.

Intervening is about helping participants see what they're doing and correct the problem. Allowing people to understand their own behavior and choose to change is can return the discussion to a productive one.

Should you intervene?

It can be hard to know when to intervene and when to let things flow naturally. The following are a few questions to consider when deciding whether or not you need to intervene.

- Is the problem a serious one?

- Will this resolve itself?

- How much time will it take to intervene? Do we have the time required?

- Will intervening cause a disruption?

- How will intervening impact the flow of the meeting and impact relationships?

- Can the intervention make things worse?

- Will anyone's self-esteem be damaged?

- Do I know the players involved well enough to intervene?

- Do I have the credibility needed with the group?

- What will happen if I do nothing?

If you do nothing and the group's progress is hindered, you will need to take action and get the group back on course.

How to Intervene.

When you realize you need to intervene, you want to make sure you use appropriate language that will promote respect and thought. You want to use objective statements about what you're observing. For example:

- I'm noticing that...

- It strikes me that...

- In my observation…

- I'd like to suggest…

- You seem to be…

You can also ask questions to allow the group to recognize what's going on by saying things like:

- What are people experiencing right now?

- How do people feel things are going at this point?

Keeping your language neutral and remaining calm will help you to intervene in a positive way and get the discussion back where it needs to be.

Asking questions is usually a better approach because people will accept their own observations. However, you may need to suggest changes or be more assertive when people aren't following ground rules.

Dealing with Resistance.

It's important to have a strategy in mind for handling a situation when the group is resistant to your facilitation efforts. There are many reasons why a group might resist such as poor timing, a meeting topic that doesn't really meet their needs, and even fear that they're taking too many risks by participating.

Sometimes you'll see resistance come out into the open while there will be other times that the resistance remains concealed verbally but can be observed through body language and facial expressions.

When you encounter resistance, you need to handle it carefully with a two-step process. Step 1 is to invite the person to share his or her resistance. You'll need to be an active listener, paraphrase their feelings, and offer empathy.

Step 2 is to ask for solutions to the barriers causing resistance. You can do this by asking questions like:

- What assurance will eliminate your concerns?

- What can the group do to support you continuing?

Most of the time resistance occurs when a person doesn't feel heard. When you allow them to vent their concerns, the resistance often fades.

What Works for You?

As you've read through these strategies, is there a specific one that makes sense for you? How can you take this information back to your own workplace and make it work for positive outcomes?

You may find that you need different strategies for different situations. Often you must experiment to find which technique rings true for you. The more you practice conflict resolution, the easier it will become.

You'll eventually develop your own style for facilitating conflict resolution and you'll become more comfortable with it.

Chapter 10: The Importance of Workplace Relationships

Almost every work environment requires the development of relationships. Sometimes these relationships are easy going and productive. But there are often struggles when you must deal with someone whose behavior is difficult.

In this chapter we'll discuss the importance of reciprocal relationships and some difficult situations that can crop up. We'll also look at appropriate ways to deal with change and use a technique called the agreement frame.

Reciprocal Relationships

In a relationship with someone else, we generally have expectations. These expectations can become self-fulfilling prophecies. For example, if you expect someone to be dishonest, you may use nonverbal expressions that make that person feel uncomfortable.

As a result he or she may actually feel like it's not okay to trust you and will keep some information hidden. Thus the person isn't honest with you. In order to prevent this, it's important to raise your expectations of people – they will usually rise to them.

You can achieve better results when you expect more from people and praise them for what they're doing right. You can also improve relationships by being aware of your own biases and break bad habits that are destructive.

It's always important to assume the best of people until they prove you otherwise. And when there are problems, it's important to have open and honest discussions to resolve the issues.

Dealing with Change

Change can be very difficult for many people while others embrace it. Think about the issues surrounding change in your own business.

What are some of the changes you ask employees or clients to make? How do they respond when asked to make those changes?

Think about why they might resist the change. What are things you need to be aware of when you're asking for change? There are several things you can do to make change more positive for those who are resistant to it.

Why Do Some Resist Change?

Some employees may feel that there's no need to change or that the change will cause more harm than good. The change may not have been presented in a positive way to begin with.

If people don't feel they were able to have input on the change, they might be more resistant to it. Change can sometimes feel like a criticism of the current work that they're doing, leading to resentment.

Changes can also create more work and if an employee is already stretched thin, there can be resistance. While you may view change as exciting and necessary, you can't expect everyone to share your view.

However, you can work to reduce resistance and improve the way change works in the workplace. Consider the following when introducing change to employees or clients.

- Ask for feedback in making the changes rather than telling people what they should do

- Treat each person with dignity and respect

- Help people understand how the change can benefit them

- Allow people to make suggestions and have input on how the change will take place – and really listen to those ideas

- Show how the change can improve the future of individuals in the group

When people can see how the change will benefit them and understand the reason behind the change, it's easier for them to get on board. Most people are happier when they feel heard and are valued enough to be asked to give input.

However, it's important that you don't ask for input that you're not going to take into consideration. Remember that your employees and clients are vast resources and can often come up with great ideas.

The Agreement Frame

When you find yourself in a situation that requires you to be very honest about changes that need to be made. This requires you to communicate the way you feel about an issue without compromising your beliefs. You also want to prevent disagreement.

There are three phrases you can use that will help you to maintain positive communication while sticking to your guns. These three questions make up the Agreement Frame.

The three phrases are:

- I appreciate and…

- I respect and…

- I agree and …

For example, "I respect the way you feel about this issue, and I think if you understood my point of view you might feel differently."

Keeping Relationships Intact

It's important that you don't allow differences in opinion or low expectations keep you from having positive relationships.

Relationships are what really build the success of a business or cause its downfall.

Think about how you can apply these strategies to foster positive relationships. In the next chapter we'll discuss change in even more detail.

Chapter 11: The Ten Commandments of Change

Sam Deep and Lyle Sussman have come up with 10 commandments related to change. You can use them for dealing with your own changes, but they're also very valuable for working with others.

In this chapter we'll take a look at these commandments and how they can benefit you. These are good general rules for working with people to make positive changes in your business or personal life.

#1 Expect the Best

You need to expect the best from people – this is how you get their best. And you shouldn't keep your expectations to yourself. Make sure you tell your employees what you expect from them.

It's so much easier to give your boss what she wants when you know what that is. You should also ask your employees what they expect from you. As a leader, it's important to meet your staff's needs.

#2 Listen Before Talking; Think Before Acting

It can be tempting to do more talking than listening, but it's important to train yourself to listen first. And instead of making impulsive decisions, you need to really think through the consequences of any actions.

Before you decide on changes or talk to your employees about the changes you need, plan what you'll say and try to adapt your message for the individual receiving it.

#3 Get to the Point

Instead of beating around the bush, be direct when you're asking for change. Don't expect people to read between the lines. When you're clear about what you want and need, you'll get better results.

Make sure that you check for understanding that your message is received and understood by your employees or clients. Having an outline of what you'd like to say will help you to do this more efficiently and effectively.

#4 Change What They Do, Not Who They Are

When you are asking for changes, make sure that you focus on changing behaviors and not changing personality traits. It's important to think about specific actions you'd like to see change. But it's not possible to ask someone to change the way they feel or their attitude.

It doesn't really matter if their personality changes as long as you get the behaviors you need to keep work a productive place. If you can learn to embrace the good parts of someone's personality and focus on behavior you'll have more success.

#5 Model What You Want

It's hard to ask your staff to change a behavior and do something if you're not also willing to model that same behavior. Leaders should be working the hardest and showing the best behaviors so that their staff has a good example to follow.

Leaders who ask their staff to behave in a specific way, yet aren't willing to model that behavior, aren't likely to get much buy in.

#6 Adapt Your Approach

As a leader, it's important that you know the people you lead. One approach might work with an employee, but fail miserably with another type of person. For example, there are some people who can handle a little humor and teasing while others feel very uncomfortable with that approach.

As you get to know your staff, you can modify your approach and get the best outcomes.

#7 Keep Dignity and Self-Respect Intact

Remember that when you're dealing with employees they are people first. It's important not to damage someone's self-respect or treat anyone with anything less than dignity. There are several phrases that you can use to keep from damaging people such as:

- I admit that I was wrong

- What is your opinion?

- Thank you

- Please

- You did a good job

These phrases remind us that we're working together at relationships with living, breathing people who have their own feelings and needs.

#8 Appeal to Self-Interest

In the end, people are more likely to make a change if they understand how it benefits them. Remember to help your employees understand how the change you're asking for will benefit them in the short-term and the long run.

As a boss it can be more comfortable to talk about what you want and need, but remember that your employees have their own wants and needs.

#9 Rejoice at Success

People often get called into their boss's office when there's a problem. But how often do we take the time to celebrate success? When your employees are working hard to make changes it's important to celebrate.

There are many ways you can do that – an email specifically outlining what you noticed, a special lunch to honor your employees, or even giving people a few hours off at the end of the day.

#10 Cut Your Losses Without Guilt

Sometimes what you want to have happen just isn't going to work out. It's important to learn from those experiences, but it doesn't do any good to dwell on them. Learn what you can and move on.

Preventing Problems

One of the best ways to keep conflict from taking over in your workplace is to prevent problems before they can take hold. It's a lot easier to prevent problems than it is to fix them once things get out of control.

Having empathy is one way that you can help employees know that you understand their feelings. This doesn't mean that you agree with them, but it does show that you care about their feelings.

Using paraphrasing is a great way to show empathy. By doing this you have the opportunity to share with your employees that you care about their feelings and you also get time to think about what you can do to respond appropriately.

Checking for Understanding

It's always important to make sure that you really understand what your employees are feeling and that they understand what you're saying to them. It's dangerous to make assumptions such as:

- People always pay attention to what you're saying

- When someone says "I know" they really know

- Repeating something over and over means that it is understood

- Saying something more slowly our loudly will make what you say more effective

- When people say they're paying attention to you, they actually are

It's important to be certain that the message is getting across. It's also important to look for cues that conflict could be on the rise. You can do this in many different ways such as:

- Looking for non-verbal communication for lack of eye contact, facial expressions, and closed body language

- Tone of voice can help you to know if someone is feeling angry, defensive, or reluctant

- Asking open questions can help you to clarify

As you get information you can make sure everyone is on the same page and avoid much of the conflict related to miscommunication. You can also get feedback from your employees which can help you to problem solve before anger and resentment comes into play.

Embracing Change

Change is hard for many people. Remember that your employees are also people and have emotions, feelings, opinions, needs, and desires. You're much more likely to get cooperation when you work with them in a way that honors their humanity.

How can you apply the lessons in this chapter to your own workplace? Have you ever had a bad experience with asking for change? What would have made it a better experience for all involved?

Chapter 12: Dealing with Difficult People

While we can work to prevent problems, we won't always be successful at doing so. Sometimes a problem will seem to have come out of nowhere. Of course, there were probably signs that we missed.

But what do you do when you suddenly are faced with conflict? In some cases you simply have to address problems and in other cases you have to learn to deal with difficult people who aren't going to make it easy for you.

Dealing with Problems

There are several strategies that can come to your aid when you're blindsided with a problem. We'll look at eight ways you can address problems without panicking.

Assess.

It's always important to think before you do anything. Many people react to difficult situations and that only makes problems worse. Make a plan. Even if doesn't go exactly the way you want, it's better than acting without thinking.

Meet Behavior Head-On.

When you experience difficult behavior, it's best to deal with it instead of trying to avoid it. Remember that avoiding often breeds resentment and causes conflict to get worse. You must deal with whatever has happened.

Stay Calm and Objective.

When you get emotional, it can make a bad problem worse quickly. It's important to stay objective and make sure you don't say anything that you might regret.

Be Up Front.

Try to deal with problems as quickly as possible and address the individual involved. The longer you wait to deal with a problem, the worse it will get. Make sure that you say what you need to say.

Two-Way Conversation.

When there's a problem, it's easy to give a lecture or present a one-sided view. But it's always more effective to give each person the chance to say what they want to say. Starting with this will make communication much easier.

You may even find that the person causing the problem has a better understanding that you thought and says things you would have said.

Look At It from Their Side.

It can really help you to put yourself in the shoes of the person with whom you're speaking. See how they're looking at the problem and have empathy for their experience.

Be Flexible.

One of the most important tools for conflict resolution is flexibility. Conflict can be a good thing that helps you to change the way things are done and make improvements. Be willing to change if necessary.

Be Tolerant.

Individuals have individual opinions. The world would be incredibly boring if everyone were the same. Embrace the differences that make life interesting.

Causes of Difficult Behavior

We've all had to deal with difficult people from time to time. It's easy to judge difficult behavior as being self-centered or cocky. But in reality, most bad behavior is rooted in fear.

People have four basic fears that can lead to bad behavior. They are:

- The fear of failure

- The fear of humiliation or embarrassment

- The fear of losing power

- The fear of rejection

These fears often cause people to behave in ways that are difficult for others and can even drive you crazy. And, chances are you've been a difficult person at one time or another.

Some of the things that make people difficult to deal with include whining, being negative, saying hurtful things, withdrawing, or disagreeing. They may use weapons such as anger, silence, or even tears to try to get what they want.

While we've spent a lot of time discussing conflict resolution, there are always people who make it very difficult to have a positive experience. For those people we need a different strategy.

The Five-Step Process

There are five steps that will work well when dealing with difficult people. Let's take a look at each one.

Step 1: Determine Your Involvement Level

The first thing you need to do is decide if you need to get involved. In some cases it may not be necessary for you to deal with someone who is being difficult. There are four questions you should ask yourself to determine your level of involvement:

1. Is this person important to you?

2. Has this happened before?

3. Does this bother you or other people?

4. Can you invest your time?

If you answer no to any of these questions, you should probably remove yourself from the situation. It may not be worth your time and effort. Not having to deal with a difficult person at all is the easiest path.

Step 2: Understand the Other Person

When someone is making life difficult, it's often hard to care much about their perspective. But if you can learn to understand them, you'll have a better ability to resolve problems. Use open-ended questions to learn more about them.

You may find out more was going on that you realized. At this point you may decide that you don't need to get involved, or you may decide to continue with conflict resolution.

Step 3: Influence His or Her Attitude

In this step you'll work to try to change the attitude or behavior of the person. You can't control them, but you may be able to have some influence that leads to change. There are three ways you can influence them:

1. Describe your own feelings and those of others

2. Explain the consequences of their behavior

3. Suggest other ways they might handle the problem

You don't need to make any type of threat. The idea here is just to share information. The other party is still responsible for their own behavior and consequences. Trying to force a change will only backfire.

Step 4: Resolve the Problem

This step can allow you to resolve the conflict. The idea is that you can find a solution. During this step you'll define what you expect for future behavior. You'll discuss possible solutions with the other person. In the end, you'll need to agree upon the best solutions.

Step 5: Recover and Go On

After you've come to an agreement, it's important to keep your attitude as positive as possible. You'll want to follow through with any commitments that you made as part of the solution.

When the difficult person changes and improves his behavior and/or attitude, it's important to recognize those positive changes.

Your Difficult People

Think about the difficult people you've encountered. Can you see what fears may have led to their poor behavior? How can you get to know someone better so that you can understand their perspective and make positive changes?

When you can have empathy and understand that the bad behavior is coming from insecurity, it makes a big difference in how you handle the situation and can help you to improve your own attitude.

Chapter 13: Change Begins with You

One of the most fundamental truths is that you can't change other people. The only person you have control over is you. It's important that you learn to make the changes on your end that will help you to have better interactions.

There are several ways you can monitor and change your own behavior so that you insure you're not the cause of conflict.

Put Yourself in Charge of You.

Instead of worrying so much about what everyone else is doing, take care of what's going on with you. You don't need to put yourself down or become a victim.

Instead pay attention to your own behavior and what's going on around you. Try to stop problems in the early stages before they escalate into something bigger.

Self-Talk.

Pay attention to what you say to yourself. Often we tell ourselves things that aren't really true and we can be especially hard on ourselves. Make sure that you're not telling yourself something that will make a situation worse.

Avoid the urge to put yourself down. Instead, focus on saying positive things and building your self-esteem. This will make you an easier person to deal with.

Be in Control.

Plan how you will handle situations before you act. Visualize the way it will go. After you handle a difficult situation, use it as an opportunity to learn. Analyze what happened. Identify what you did well and what you could do to improve the next time.

Once a difficult situation has been dealt with, try to put it aside. If you have leftover anger, focus the energy on positive tasks such as cleaning out your office or going for a walk.

Have a Sense of Humor.

If you can laugh about difficulties that happen in life, you'll naturally be happier. Laughter can help you to reduce stress levels, relax, and give you a more positive outlook on life.

Use Your Support Team.

When you face challenges, it's incredibly important to have support. You need to develop a solid team of people who can rally around you when you need support. And in turn you can give them support.

Who do you have in your office and your home life that can help you to get through difficult times? It's important to also remember that when you should avoid gossip or sharing confidential information with someone in the workplace.

Why Don't People Just Do What They're Supposed to Do?

You've probably had many encounters with difficult people and wondered why they couldn't just do what they were supposed to do. There can be many reasons for this and it may help you to think about some of those reasons.

Research shows that there are common reasons why behavior doesn't always meet our expectations. People don't always do what they're supposed to do because…

- They didn't know why they should do it

- They didn't know when to start and stop it

- They didn't know what they were really supposed to do

- They didn't know how to do what they were supposed to do

- They thought they were doing it already

- They thought their way was better than your way

- They had different priorities

- They weren't rewarded for doing it

- There were no consequences for not doing it

- They didn't believe they could do it

Think of a time when you didn't do what you were supposed to do. No one is perfect and you've certainly been in that situation. Even if you were trying hard you might not have met expectations. What were the reasons behind that failure?

Remember that each person has his or her own perspective. It's important to communicate to make sure that everyone understands what's expected.

Beginning with your own behavior sets the tone for the entire workplace. When you control your own behavior and work not to be a difficult person yourself, you can have a huge influence on the people around you.

What Do You Need to Change?

We all have things about our personalities or behavior we'd like to change. What are some things you can work on right now that will make it easier for people to communicate with you and work with you?

Make it a goal to work on those things and pay attention to your own journey. You'll find it much easier to deal with other people when you're willing to take responsibility for your own actions.

Chapter 14: Don't Let Anger Get the Best of You

No matter how hard you work on your own behavior, you're still human. Human beings can get angry, but in this day and age it seems like too many people are angry in the workplace.

This leads to workplace violence in extreme situations, but more often than not it doesn't escalate to that point. However, anger can cause teamwork to dissolve and reduce productivity.

It can lead to a hostile environment that's negative and can even be frightening for some people. Instead of work being a place where you can have fun, feel comfortable, and excel it can become a place that you dread going to each day.

It's not possible to eliminate all anger from the workplace because anger is a natural, human emotion. But you can do a lot toward creating an environment where anger isn't allowed to breed. Anger management is key to creating a healthy workplace.

But many people aren't really trained in anger management. One thing you can do to improve your workplace is provide training in anger management so that people understand appropriate ways to deal with this normal emotion.

Managing Your Own Anger

Anger itself isn't the problem. Rather, the problem comes when anger is expressed in inappropriate ways. Some positive ways that anger can be managed include:

- Expressing your feelings appropriately

- Releasing physical tension with exercise

- Analyzing the cause of your anger

- Addressing your fear

- Putting yourself in charge of you

- Using logic to approach the situation

Some negative behaviors that escalate anger include:

- Accusing others of making you angry

- Bringing up the past to fight today's battles

- Preaching at others when you're angry and feel out of control

- Name calling

- Throwing or hitting objects or people

- Yelling and screaming

All of these behaviors can make angry feelings even more intense and can cause bigger problems than you were already experiencing. Instead, try some alternatives that will help you calm down and get some perspective.

Some positive ways to manage your anger include:

- Going for a walk to burn off physical energy

- Yelling in the woods instead of yelling at someone else

- Write an angry letter that you'll never send – say whatever negative things you're thinking and feeling

- Write a constructive letter describing the problem and deliver it – ask the recipient to read it and plan a time to talk when you cool off

- Take some time to practice deep breathing – even just a minute or two can help you to calm down

These things can all be helpful when your own angry feelings are causing you to see stars. As you calm down you'll be able to make more rational decisions and use appropriate behavior. Sometimes you just need to remove yourself from the situation at hand to get perspective.

Dealing with Other People's Anger

Sometimes our own anger isn't the problem. If you're dealing with someone else who is angry, it's important to remember your own behavior. Do your best to keep the situation from escalating and getting out of control.

It's important to remember to use positive self-talk. Don't put yourself down and stoop to the other person's level. Also make sure that you use positive body language so that you appear interested and relaxed.

When someone is anger, they often just want to be heard. Use active listening and acknowledge the other person's feelings. At the same time be willing to be vulnerable and share your own feelings.

Express what you need and want in a calm way. You may need to repeat yourself a few times in order for the angry person to hear what you're saying. Remember that when you're dealing with someone who is angry, he or she may have low self-esteem.

Complimenting them or building them up can be a way to break the anger cycle and change the conversation. Avoid arguing with someone who is angry, even though they may put pressure on you to do so.

If you've done something to hurt the person who is angry, make sure to take responsibility and apologize. Sometimes that's all the other person really wants out of the conversation.

Expressing Anger Appropriately and Assertively

If you're experiencing anger, it's important to know how you can address an issue with a coworker (or even someone in your personal life) in order to resolve conflict and move forward positively.

Begin by being positive.

Instead of launching into all of your frustrations, begin by sincerely letting your coworker know what you appreciate about them. Then you can let them know about your feelings.

For example: "I've really enjoyed working with you over the past few months on this project. Lately I have been feeling that there is some tension between us because…"

Be Direct.

When you're trying to discuss an issue it can be confusing if you're not direct about it. Make sure to use "I" statements, but be direct about your feelings. For example: "I feel angry as a result of …."

It's hard to resolve a conflict when you aren't willing to tell the other party about your true feelings or describe what they've done to affect you.

Be Specific About Your Anger Intensity.

When you're angry, it's helpful to tell the other party how angry you are. You could be slightly annoyed or you could be furious. Be clear about where your anger lies.

Giving the other person this information helps them to understand the impact of their behavior on you. This helps them to make decisions about their own behavior and what they need to do.

No One Makes You Angry.

When you say to someone that they "make" you angry it can cause more problems. That gives the other person too much power over your feelings.

Instead say, "I feel angry when you..." This is a better description of the way you feel coupled with the behavior that's related to it. You don't want to hand over your power to someone else. Remember that some people take pleasure in your anger.

Share Your Feelings about Fear.

When you're talking to someone about your anger it can be beneficial to let them know it makes you nervous. For example, "I'm nervous about saying this to you because you might think I am petty."

When you share your feelings you actually can feel empowered and in more control. You keep fear from paralyzing you and keeping you from taking care of your own needs. Usually sharing honest feelings will help the other person to have a more productive discussion.

Take Responsibility for Your Part.

In any conflict situation, there are usually two people who are to blame. Take responsibility for your own part of the problem. For example, "I should have said something earlier about this issue."

You may need to acknowledge your own poor angry behavior or overreaction. Taking responsibility for your own actions can diffuse a hostile situation.

Don't Invite Criticism.

You may be tempted to put yourself down or criticize yourself. But this can actually cause more anger and problems. Avoid this urge as it may open you up to more criticism and anger from the other party.

Protecting Yourself from Criticism.

When someone is heavily criticizing you, it's important to protect yourself. You may need to acknowledge that there is some truth to what the person is saying. However, this doesn't mean you need to accept abusive behavior and comments.

You can also try the technique called "broken record". With this technique you repeat the same statement over and over again in a calm voice. You can also agree with the criticism without adding your own put downs.

Reducing Your Own Stress

Stress reduction can be a powerful weapon against anger. Try these techniques for relaxing the body and mind so that you can reduce the effects of stress. This will help you to feel happier and healthier and will reduce your risk of conflict.

Deep Breathing.

Deep breathing, also known as belly breathing, can help you to release tension in your body and calm your mind. You don't need any training in order to perform this.

Find a comfortable position and breathe in slowly. When you breathe in hold your breath for one or two seconds then slowly release it. You can repeat this a few times and feel the tension leaving your body.

What's nice about deep breathing is that you can do it almost anywhere. While sitting at your desk you can take a few deep breaths. You can even escape to a restroom to have a moment to yourself for deep breathing.

Visualization.

You can also use positive imagery to help you become more confident and positive. Visualize the place where you feel most at peace. You can carry that visualization with you anywhere to return to the peaceful feelings you associate with it.

Music.

Music is a powerful tool when it comes to changing your mood. You can use relaxing music to help calm your body and mind. You can also use music to boost your energy levels and help you to feel more positive.

Music can be the perfect pick me up when you're feeling tired and need a boost. It can also help you to find peace when tensions start to rise.

Exercise.

Stress often settles in the body through sore and tight muscles. Exercise can help you to release tension.

You don't have to work out to the point of exhaustion. Even taking a daily walk can help you to release the tension from the day and feel better.

Acupressure.

Acupressure is a technique that can help to open energy pathways in your body. Similar to acupuncture points, you can apply pressure to the same points and get relief even if you're sitting at your desk. This can relieve headache pain and other types of muscle tension.

Massage.

Massaging your neck and head can help to relieve stress. However, we all know it feels better when someone else gives you a massage. Try going to a massage therapist regularly or ask a friend or spouse to help massage tension areas.

Laughter.

You've heard the saying that laughter is the best medicine, and research suggests that it is true. Laughter can help to lower your blood pressure, ease tight muscles, and can even slow down your body's adrenaline production.

Make sure you have a stash of funny movies and books to lift your spirits. You can also spend time with friends and family who help you to find laughter in your life.

Positive Affirmations.

When you speak positively, you can improve your outlook, reduce your stress, and have healthier relationships. You might try writing them down on cards and keeping them in places where you can see them.

You may even want to record some affirmations on your phone and play them when you're experiencing a moment of stress. Here are a few ideas to get you started:

- Getting upset won't help the situation

- I'm in control of my own actions

- I can't change anyone else, I can only change myself

- Stay calm

- Relax and let go

- Make no judgments

- Anger won't solve anything

- I'm worth taking care of

- I can't expect people to do what I want them to do

- I don't have to take this situation so seriously

By working to release your own tension you can manage your anger better. It will also help you to learn to stay calm when others are trying to cause problems or conflict begins to lead to tension.

Conclusion

In this guide you've learned what conflict is, how it develops, and how you can work to resolve conflict in any situation. You've also learned how to improve your own communication so that you can prevent problems from becoming worse.

Start with Your Own Behavior

It's easy to point the finger at someone else when conflict arises, but the only person you can change is you. Make sure that you always look at your own behavior first. When you're in control, you can often keep situations from escalating.

Remember that most conflict isn't personal. It's really about the feelings and fears of the other person. With active listening you can begin to understand the other parties involved and problem solve so that everyone can be happy.

Conflict Can Be Good

Don't forget that conflict gives you opportunities to become more creative, understand a new perspective, and improve processes in the workplace. When you embrace conflict rather than trying to avoid it you'll have fewer problems.

You may want to take your knowledge and offer training to your employees so that you can all be on the same page about how to handle conflict in your office culture.

If you're dealing with a lot of conflict in your workplace, look at the norms in your office. You may need to have a discussion about ground rules and how to approach communication more positively.

And remember that as a leader, your example is more important than the words you say. When you show appropriate behavior and respect toward others, you'll be more likely to get buy in from your employees and coworkers.

Next Steps

Once you've spent some time improving your conflict resolution skills, you may find that there are other areas in your workplace that could use work.

If you're struggling with being assertive in the workplace and you need to increase your confidence, you'll want to read **"Workplace Solutions: Unlocking Your Potential with Self-Esteem and Positive Communication"**. This guide will give you more depth on dealing with these issues that we only touched upon in this volume.

It's important to be able to have balance and not be obnoxious at work, but you also need to be able to speak up on matters that count, make a contribution, and make sure that your voice is heard when it is time for promotions and raises to be handed out. If you don't feel self confident, and you don't use appropriate assertiveness in your communications to promote yourself, then who else will do it for you?

You may also find that as a leader in your business, it's time to pass on some of your motivation to your workforce.

In **"Workplace Solutions: Motivating Your Workforce and Negotiating for Results"** you'll get in depth information on how you can motivate your workforce. You'll also learn key negotiation skills so that you can develop the ability to get what you need while growing your business.

When your corporate workforce is motivated and has good negotiation skills, you'll see a huge improvement in the culture of your business as well as its profits.

Here is an extract of this book that you might find interesting, and it gives you a sample of what is in this book:

Chapter 5: Creating a Motivational Climate

Now that you understand how important motivation is and know some of the components needed, it's time to start creating a motivational climate in your own office. But how do you get started?

The Importance of a Motivational Climate

You can have the best and brightest staff, but if your organization lacks a motivational climate you won't have the success you're capable of having. Often the employee gets blamed for not caring or investing enough in his or her work.

But the truth is that the fault usually lies with the leader who didn't create a climate that was motivational and brought out the best in his or her employees. It's really up to you as a manager or other type of leader to create a place where everyone can show up and give their best.

Praise vs. Criticism

Everyone enjoys getting praise and positive feedback at work. It almost doesn't matter who gives the praise or what it's for. Praise makes you feel that you've achieved success and that others see you as capable and competent.

On the flip side, criticism and negative feedback can feel defeating. You may feel your self-esteem decrease and you may even lose interest in what you're doing. It can be a major factor in demotivating someone.

Often in a workplace environment we're quick to criticize and point out mistakes. But we can be very good at overlooking positive accomplishments. It's important that you don't spend all your time focusing on negatives.

You should spend most of your time pointing out what people are doing well. Give them positive feedback, congratulate them when they've accomplished a goal (this is one reason why you need to know their goals), and catch them doing great things.

There are many ways you can reward people for doing a great job – and they don't require a ton of energy or resources. For example:

- Spotlight in the company newsletter

- A quick email with what you've observed

- Memo that goes out to all the staff

- Bulletin board note

- A personal note

- Giving more responsibility

- Promoting

There are some important things to know about giving praise. Praise is a wonderful tool and can provide great motivation when it's used correctly. But you shouldn't just throw out praise that hasn't been earned.

For one thing, your employees will feel that your praise is generic and insincere. Sending an email to the entire staff saying they are "doing a great job" is almost meaningless.

What people really want is to know that you see them. You see each person's individual contributions and you're appreciative of them. When you give praise, be specific about what it is you admire about their work.

For example, "I just wanted to let you know that the report you turned in was very well done. Your research was thorough and you made your points clearly and concisely. I look forward to more great work like this! Well done!"

It's not just a "good job". It's about being specific and really being observant. The hardest part about changing your praise into the appropriate form will be changing your own behavior.

If you're not used to seeing the good that people do and acknowledging it, you'll need to have a change of heart. It will have to be very conscious at first. The good news is that it feels just as good to give praise as it does to receive it.

Once you've got the hang of it, it becomes really easy to see all the good things going on in your office. This helps to create motivation, productivity, and a friendly climate.

And when you spend most of your time giving praise, constructive criticism doesn't hurt so much. If someone isn't performing well, start by sharing with them what they're doing right. Then let them know the specific behaviors you'd like to see improve.

It's much easier to handle criticism when it's balanced with acknowledgment of what you're doing right. Most people aren't doing everything wrong.

They may just need to make a few changes. But when you're met only with criticism, it can negate everything you do and lower your self-esteem.

Should You Praise Mediocre Work?

You don't want to praise people for mediocre work. However, you don't need to see perfect work in order to see the good that an employee is doing. You can look at progress. When someone makes improvements, note that as praiseworthy.

Mediocre work provides you with an opportunity to work with an employee to develop goals that will improve it. As those goals are met, there are many opportunities for praise. And that praise can actually lead to better motivation to do even better work.

The Expectancy Theory of Motivation

The expectancy theory of motivation is all about weighing the costs and benefits of specific actions. The theory assumes that people will be influenced by these factors when they're faced with the need to make a behavioral decision.

People will generally select the choice that has the greatest expected outcome. They'll weigh the positive minus the negative outcomes in this case. The one with the best outcome has "motivating potential" and motivates their choice.

Can you think of any situations in your experience when someone's behavior could have been explained by this theory?

As a supervisor, you can harness the power of this theory and use it to increase your employees' motivation. The idea is that if you help people to see more value in accomplishing their goals they'll be more likely to have motivation.

You can do this by pointing out some of the benefits of accomplishing specific tasks. For example, you could share that a specific type of work can lead to a promotion.

Needs vs. Risks

In general, people have four basic needs that can motivate them to make progress. When you can appeal to those needs, you can help people to see the value in their work in a way that's motivational. These needs can often dictate the types of risks a person is willing to take.

Need for Achievement.

Many people have a desire to accomplish goals. They feel the internal desire for challenge and accomplishment. This alone can drive them to great success. People who have this need find it important to set goals that are difficult, but attainable.

Someone who has this need will be willing to take calculated risks. They know something might be hard, but they're willing to give it a try. They'll need to be pretty certain they can reach their goal in order to take a risk.

Need for Power.

The ability to have authority and be a decision-maker is motivating for people who have the need for power. Sharing that work can lead to a position as a manager or supervisor can be highly motivating.

Someone with a need for power is willing to take risks if the payoff is more authority, responsibility, or a better title.

Need for Affiliation.

For some people feeling accepted and part of a group is very important. This need can be met with projects that require teamwork. When an employee feels they're part of something bigger than themselves, motivation will follow.

People with the need for affiliation are more likely to take risks when they don't have to do it on their own. Working together in a group effort is more motivating. This is the type of person that does well with an exercise buddy when they set a fitness goal.

In corporate life, this person is a team player that is motivated by fitting in and having the opportunity to share ideas.

Need to Avoid Failure.

This need is pretty self-explanatory. This can help motivate people toward success. But it can also keep people from really pushing or challenging themselves if they fear they may not be successful.

For this need, it's best to work with goals that stretch someone, but are very realistic and can be accomplished. Starting with small, simple goals can help build successes that lead to motivation. Someone who has a need to avoid failure may not be willing to take big risks.

Do You Use Praise?

Think about your own behavior as a supervisor. Do you spend much time praising your employees? Chances are, unless you're very conscious of it, you probably spend more time being critical. That just seems to be human nature.

But if you want to create a motivational climate, you need to start helping your employees to see their successes and celebrate with them. Think about something you can do within the next week to add this layer of motivation to your organization.

It's also important that you understand what needs you have that help motivate you as well as what needs motivate your employees. This can help you to make decisions about assignments and projects you can implement to meet those needs.

End of extract

This series of self help guides for the workplace will continue to grow over the years, as I will keep writing and publishing more books on the biggest issues that have been most pressing and difficult to deal with in my many decades of career development and entrepreneurship.

You can stay up to date with my latest book releases by checking out my author page here:
http://www.amazon.com/Helene-Malmsio/e/B00AO4QX6C/

I invite you to share your thoughts on my books, by posting your reader reviews at Amazon, or wherever you purchased this short report Guide or one of my books.

Over the past few years I have also been working on my own wiki style DIY website where I share my knowledge and hope to help others grow their skills, so please do drop by sometime and say hello. You will see a "contact me" form on there, so that you can share your thoughts with me, or even create your own pages online at www.learn-how-to-do-it.com

So now it only remains for me to wish you every success in your endeavors and that you also achieve the balance in life and work to be able to enjoy it fully!

Helene Malmsio

– Strategic Services and Strategic Alliances